Old Coast Guard Stations

VOLUME TWO

North Carolina

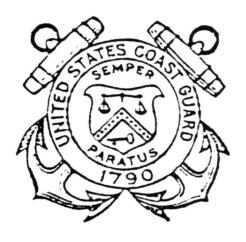

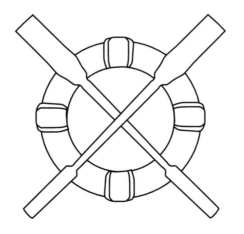

Richard L. Chenery III

Library of Congress Control Number: 00-090394
ISBN: 0-9665204-1-6

Published by:
Station Books
P.O. Box 2714
Glen Allen, Virginia 23058-2714

Printed by:
The Dietz Press
Richmond, VA

Cover designs:
(upper) U. S. Coast Guard seal (early design)
(lower) U. S. Coast Guard Surfman insignia

For my wife
LUCY TYLER

TABLE OF CONTENTS

Contributors vii

Introduction 1

Old Lifeboat Stations 10

Mirlo Rescue – 1918 81

Kyzikes Rescue – 1927 85

Anna May Rescue – 1931 85

Empire Gem Rescue – 1942 88

MV *Norfolk* Rescue – 1948 91

Omar Babun Rescue – 1954 95

British Cemeteries 98

August 4th Races 103

Conclusion 114

References 115

Index 117

CONTRIBUTORS

Thanks and deep appreciation are expressed to each and every one of the following contributors whose photographs, information, recollections, kind words and other help all made this book possible.

EN1 (L) John E. Sterling, USCG (deceased) – Onancock, VA
LCDR Dalton Burrus, USCG (ret.), and wife Ruby – Chesapeake, VA
Scott Price, Historian, USCG Headquarters – Washington, DC
Jack and Mary Huber – Richmond, VA
Joe Mobley, N C Dept. of Cultural Resources – Raleigh, NC
Ulysses L. "Mack" Womack – Ocracoke, NC
Leta Styron – Beaufort, NC
Stacy Davis – Harkers Island, NC
BMC Reginald Lewis, USCG (ret.) and wife Madeline – Harkers Island, NC
Norris W. Austin – Corolla, NC
Howard C. Lockerman – Houston, TX
Gerald Brebner, U.S. Coast Guard (ret.) – Altantic Beach, NC
BMCM Wayne Gray, U.S. Coast Guard (ret.) – Nags Head, NC
Joseph Malat, North Carolina Aquarium – Manteo, NC
BMC (L) Sheldon O'Neal, U.S. Coast Guard (ret.) – Manteo, NC
BMC Sidney C. Toler, U.S. Coast Guard (ret.) – Kitty Hawk, NC
Doug Twiddy, Twiddy & Co. Realtors – Duck, NC
Gayle Sanders, Twiddy & Co. Realtors – Corolla, NC
Wynne Dough, Outer Banks History Center – Manteo, NC
Lois Bradshaw, Outer Banks History Center – Manteo, NC
Steve Harrison, National Park Service, Cape Hatteras Group – Manteo, NC
Robert E. Huggett, Chicamacomico Historical Association – Rodanthe, NC
BM1 "Tink" Scarborough, U.S. Coast Guard (ret.) – Kill Devil Hills, NC
Theodore Mutro – Ocracoke, NC
William Dough – Manteo, NC
Del Agee – Richmond, VA
EN1 Johnny Williams, USCG (ret.) – Buxton, NC
LCDR Lenwood M. Quidley, USCG (ret.) – Hatteras, NC
CBM Erving Gray, USCG (ret.), and wife Mary – Elizabeth City, NC
Wendy Strickland – Outer Banks History Center – Manteo, NC

INTRODUCTION

The origin of United States Coast Guard assistance to mariners in distress from lifeboat stations can be traced back to the 1870's when the United States Life-Saving Service started building stations to house crews and their boats and equipment to be available when needed for rescue. When the Coast Guard was formed in 1915 by the merger of the Life-Saving Service with the Revenue Cutter-Service the Coast Guard took over the operation of those stations. During the period leading up to World War II (1915-41) the Coast Guard continued operating many of them, closed some stations, rebuilt some in better locations, and added some new stations.

Stations were originally built along the coast at regular intervals (often every seven miles) so that the surfmen assigned to each station could patrol the beach on foot and reach wrecked vessels in rowed surfboats. Back in the 19th century, in the waning days of the age of sail and before invention of radio, helicopters and all the other modern means of communication and fast travel, the emphasis was on aiding mariners in distress on sailing vessels wrecked near shore stations.

Whenever shipwrecks occurred the station crews had to pull a surfboat on a beach wagon (manually or with horses or mules) across the beach and launch the boat into the surf. At some of the inlet stations they could launch boats from a carriage down a launchway. They would then row out to the vessel and try to save everyone on board. If the wreck were close enough inshore, they would throw a line out to the wreck using a Lyle gun and rig a breeches buoy to bring people ashore.

The waters off the entire coast of North Carolina, from Currituck Beach southward down past Cape Hatteras and on down to Cape Lookout and Cape Fear, have always been very treacherous to mariners. Shallow, constantly shifting shoals reach far out from shore off Cape Hatteras and both the Gulf Stream and the Labrador Current pass the coast here, all of which makes these waters some of the most dangerous in the world. For good reasons this area has come to be known as The Graveyard of the Atlantic. Over two thousand ships have gone down here. The twenty-nine lifeboat stations built along the North Carolina coast were needed in days gone by, but over the years their numbers have been scaled back as conditions changed and new methods and technology evolved.

This book tells just a small part of the heroic story of those iron men and their wooden boats at the old North Carolina stations in the early years of the Coast Guard, 1915 – 1955. Beginning with the Life-Saving Service in the 1870's and continuing in the Coast Guard up until 1939, men at the shore stations were rated as

Boat equipment of Coast Guard stations.

ATLANTIC AND GULF COASTS.

Name of station.	District No.	Power boats. Lifeboats. 34-foot.	36-foot.	Power boats. Surfboats. Beebe-McLellan.	Beebe open.	Miscellaneous.	Without engine power, surfboats. Beebe-McLellan.	Beebe, open.	Monomoy.	Other.	Miscellaneous. Dinghys, dories.	Supply boats.
Absecon, N. J.	5						2	1				
Amagansett, N. Y.	4							2				
Aransas, Tex.	9				1		1			1	1	1
Assateague Beach, Va.	6	1		1			3					
Atlantic City, N. J.	5			1			3					
Avalon, N. J.	5						2					
Barnegat, N. J.	5	1		1			2			1		
Bay Head, N. J.	5						1			1		
Bellport, N. Y.	4						1	1				
Bethany Beach, Del.	6						2		1		1	
Bethel Creek, Fla.[1]	8											
Big Kinnakeet, N. C.	7						1			1	1	
Biscayne Bay, Fla.[1]	8					1						
Block Island, R. I.	3							2			1	
Blue Point, N. Y.	4				1		1	1				
● Bodie Island, N. C.	7						1				1	
● Bogue Inlet, N. C.	7				1		1				1	
Bonds, N. J.	5						2					
Brant Rock, Mass.	2								2	1	2	
Brazos, Tex.	9				1		1			1	1	1
Brenton Point, R. I.	3		1				1				1	
Brigantine, N. J.	5				1		1					
Bulow, Fla.[1]	8											
Burnt Island, Me.	1					1			1	1	2	
● Caffeys Inlet, N. C.	7						1			1	1	
Cahoons Hollow, Mass.	2								2		1	
Cape Elizabeth, Me.	1			1					1	2	2	
● Cape Fear, N. C.	7				1		1				1	
● Cape Hatteras, N. C.	7				1		1			1		1
Cape Henlopen, Del.	6						3					
Cape Henry, Va.	7				1		2					
● Cape Lookout, N. C.	7		1				1				1	
Cape May, N. J.	5				1		2					
Cedar Creek, N. J.	5											
Chadwick, N. J.	5						1					
Chatham, Mass.	2									3	2	
Chester Shoal, Fla.[1]	8										1	
● Chicamacomico, N. C.	7				1		1			1		
City Point, Mass.	2					2²				3³		
Cobb Island, Va.	6	1					1			1	1	
Cold Spring, N. J.	5						2					
● Core Bank, N. C.	7				1		1			1		
Corson Inlet, N. J.	5						2					
Coskata, Mass.	2				1		1			1	1	4
Cranberry Islands, Me.	1					1					3	1
● Creeds Hill, N. C.	7				1		1				2	
Cross Island, Me.	1				1					2	1	1
● Currituck Beach, N. C.	7				1		1					
Cuttyhunk, Mass.	2		1		1					3	1	
Damiscove Island, Me.	1		1	1						1	2	2
Dam Neck Mills, Va.	7						1					
● Deal, N. C.	5						1					
Ditch Plain, N. Y.	4						1	1				
● Durants, N. C.	7						1			1		
Eatons Neck, N. Y.	4				1		1				1	
False Cape, Va.	7				1		1					
Fenwick Island, Del.	6				1					1	1	
Fire Island, N. Y.	4				1		1	1			1	
Fishers Island, N. Y.	3				1		1				1	
Fletchers Neck, Me.	1								1	2	1	
Forge River, N. Y.	4						1	1				
Forked River, N. J.	5				1		2			1		
Fort Lauderdale, Fla.[1]	8										1	
● Fort Macon, N. C.	7				1		1				1	
Fourth Cliff, Mass.	2				1					1	1	
Galveston, Tex.	9		1		1		1			1	1	

[1] House of refuge. [2] Launches; also 1 steam tug. [3] Whitehall rowboats.

1915 station list - pages from the *Annual Report of the United States Coast Guard,* fiscal year ended June 30, 1915. Note that inlet stations (Cape Lookout, Hatteras Inlet, and Oak Island) all have 36-foot motor lifeboats but that many of the beach stations have no power boats at all. (U.S. Coast Guard)

Boat equipment of Coast Guard stations—Continued.

ATLANTIC AND GULF COASTS—Continued.

Name of station.	District No.	Power boats.					Without engine power, surfboats.				Miscellaneous.	
		Lifeboats.		Surfboats.			Beebe-McLellan.	Beebe, open.	Monomoy.	Other.	Dinghys, dories.	Supply boats.
		34-foot.	36-foot.	Beebe-McLellan.	Beebe, open.	Miscellaneous.						
Gay Head, Mass	2			1			1		2	1	1	
Georgica, N. Y.	4						1	1				1
Gilberts Bar, Fla.¹	8										1	
Gilgo, N. Y.	4						1					
Gloucester, Mass	2		1				1				1	2
Great Egg, N. J.	5				1		1					1
Great Wass Island, Me	1					1					3	2
Green Hill, R. I.	3						1	1			1	1
Green Run Inlet, Md	6				1		1		1		1	
Gull Shoal, N. C.	7						1				2	
Gurnet, Mass	2			1	1		1			1	1	
Hampton Beach, N. H.	1								1		2	1
Harvey Cedars, N. J.	5						2					
Hatteras Inlet, N. C.	5	1					1				1	
Hereford Inlet, N. J.	5			1			2	1				
High Head, Mass	2									2	2	1
Highland, Mass	2								2		1	1
Hither Plain, N. Y.	4							1	1			
Hog Island, Va	6	1		1	1		1					
Holly Beach, N. J.	5						2					
Hunniwells Beach, Me	1				1		1				3	1
Indian River Inlet, Del	6						1		1		1	
Indian River Inlet, Fla.¹	8								1			
Island Beach, N. J.	5						2					
Isle of Wight, Md	6						1		1		1	1
Isles of Shoals, Me	1	1							1	1	2	1
Jones Beach, N. Y.	4						1	1				
Kill Devil Hills, N. C.	7						1				1	
Kitty Hawk, N. C.	7						1				1	
Lewes, Del	6	1	1						1			
Little Beach, N. J.	5				1		1					
Little Egg, N. J.	5			1			1		1		1	
Little Island, Va	7						1	1				
Little Kinnakeet, N. C.	7						2					
Lone Hill, N. Y.	4						1	2				
Long Beach, N. Y.	4						1	2				
Long Beach, N. J.	5						2					
Long Branch, N. J.	5						1			1		
Loveladies Island, N. J.	5						1					
Maddaket, Mass	2			1					1	1	2	1
Manomet Point, Mass	2								1	1	1	
Mantoloking, N. J.	5					1	1					3
Mecox, N. Y.	4						1		1			
Metomkin Inlet, Va	6			1	1		1				1	1
Monmouth Beach, N. J.	5								2		1	3
Monomoy, Mass	2		1		1				2	1		2
Monomoy Point, Mass	2			1			2		1			
Moriches, N. Y.	4					1	1	1				
Mosquito Lagoon, Fla.¹	8						1				1	
Muskeget, Mass	2				1		1				2	2
Nags Head, N. C.	7						1	1				
Nahant, Mass	2								1	1	1	2
Napeague, N. Y.	4						1	2				
Narragansett Pier, R. I.	3					1	1	1				1
Nauset, Mass	2								2	2	1	2
Newburyport, Mass	2			1			1				1	
New Inlet, N. C.	7										1	
New Shoreham, R. I.	3							2				1
North Beach, Md	6						1	1				
North Scituate, Mass	2						1				2	1
Oak Island, N. Y.	4						1	1				
Oak Island, N. C.	7	1					1					
Ocean City, N. J.	5				1		1					
Ocean City, Md	6				1		1				1	
Ocracoke, N. C.	7				1		2		1			
Old Harbor, Mass	2								2		1	
Oregon Inlet, N. C.	7						1				1	

¹ House of refuge.

1915 Station list, cont.

Boat equipment of Coast Guard stations—Continued.

ATLANTIC AND GULF COASTS—Continued.

Name of station.	District No.	Power boats. Lifeboats. 34-foot.	36-foot.	Power boats. Surfboats. Beebe-McLellan.	Beebe, open.	Miscellaneous.	Without engine power, surfboats. Beebe-McLellan.	Beebe, open.	Monomoy.	Other.	Miscellaneous. Dinghys, dories.	Supply boats.
Orleans, Mass	2			1						3	1	
Pamet River, Mass	2								1	2	1	
Parramore Beach, Va	6			1	1		1					
● Paul Gamiels Hill, N. C	7						1					
● Pea Island, N. C	7						1					
Peaked Hill Bars, Mass	2						1				2	
Pecks Beach, N. J	5						2				2	1
● Penneys Hill, N. C	7			1			2					
Plum Island, Mass	2			1			1					
Point Allerton, Mass	2		1		1		1			2	2	
Point Judith, R. I	3						1	1	1		1	3
Point Lookout, N. Y	4				1		1	1				
Point of Woods, N. Y	4				1		1	1			1	1
Popes Island, Va	6						2					1
● Portsmouth, N. C	7	1					1					
Portsmouth Harbor, Me	1			1					1		2	2
Potunk, N. Y	4						1	1			2	
● Poyners Hill, N. C	7						1			1	2	
Quoddy Head, Me	1						1			1	2	2
Quogue, N. Y	4						1	1			2	
Quonochontaug, R. I	3						1	1			2	
Race Point, Mass	2				1		1			2	1	
Rehoboth Beach, Del	6						1		1		1	
Rockaway, N. Y	4							2				
Rockaway Point, N. Y	4				1		1					
Rocky Point, N. Y	4			1			1	2				
Rye Beach, N. H	1								1	2	1	
Sabine Pass, Tex	9				1	1	1			1	1	1
Salisbury Beach, Mass	2								1	1	3	
Saluria, Tex	9								2		1	1
Sandy Hook, N. J	5		1	1		1	1					
Sandy Point, R. I	3						1	1			1	
San Luis, Tex	9				1		1					1
Santa Rosa, Fla	9			1	1		2		1	2	1	1
Seabright, N. J	5					1	1				1	
Sea Isle City, N. J	5						1					
Shark River, N. J	5						1			1		
Shinnecock, N. Y	4				1		1	1				
Ship Bottom, N. J	5						2					
Short Beach, N. Y	4	1					1	1				
Smith Island, Pa	6		1				1		1			
Smiths Point, N. Y	4				1		1		1		1	
Southampton, N. Y	4								2		1	
South Brigantine, N. J	5			1			1					
Spermaceti Cove, N. J	5			1			1					
Spring Lake, N. J	5			1			1					
Squan Beach, N. J	5						2					
Stone Harbor, N. J	5			1			1					
Straitsmouth, Mass	2			1			1					
Sullivans Island, S. C	8			1			1		1	1	1	
Surfside, Mass	2								1	1	1	
Tiana, N. Y	4						1	1				
Toms River, N. J	5					1	1				1	
Townsend Inlet, N. J	5						1					
Two Mile Beach, N. J	5			1			1					
Velasco, Tex	9						1		2		1	1
Virginia Beach, Va	7				1		1				1	
Wachapreague, Va	6	1					1				1	
Wallis Sands, N. H	1									2	2	
Wallops Beach, Va	6				1		2					
● Wash Woods, N. C	7			1			2					
Watch Hill, R. I	3		1		1		1	1			1	
White Head, Me	1					1				4	2	
Wood End, Mass	2		1						1	2	1	
Zachs Inlet, N. Y	4						1	1				

[1] Ice scooter.

1915 Station list, cont.

surfmen. A surfman wore a distinctive dress uniform which included a hat with a visor, white shirt and tie, coat and trousers — as opposed to a cutterman's sailor hat, jumper and bell bottom trousers. The surfman's work uniform was dungarees, chambray shirt and the hat. A surfman's hat included a device consisting of a ring buoy and two crossed oars, blades up. Surfmen were in the Lifesaving Branch of the Coast Guard and could advance to boatswain's mate or motor machinist's mate (engineman after 1947). They were given an "L" designator and were known as "L" men. By the end of the1950's they all had either advanced to chief petty officer or warrant officer or had been commissioned or had retired, and the old surfman rating passed into history.

Winter uniform coat, surfman (rated BM1c). This coat and other interesting USLSS and USCG memorabilia are on display at the Twiddy and Company Realtors office in Corolla next to the gift shop which was once Kill Devil Hills Lifesaving Station. (author)

NORFOLK DISTRICT

Norfolk, Va.

Capt. Thaddius G. Crapster, district commander
Commander Russell L. Lucas, chief of staff

COAST GUARD PATROL

MENDOTA: Commander Leo C. Mueller.
HAMILTON: Commander Stephen S. Yeandle.
BIBB: Commander Joseph E. Stika.
SEBAGO: Commander Nobel G. Ricketts.

MODOC: Lt. Comdr. Harold G. Belford.
DIONE: Lt. Quentin M. Greeley.
CALYPSO: Lt. W. C. Capron.
McLANE: Chief Boatswain John L. Olsen.

DISTRICT VESSELS

PAMLICO: Lt. Herman T. Diehl.
CGC 22, 228.
CARRABASSET: Chief Boatswain Clarence W. Whitney.
CALUMET: Chief Boatswain Samuel D. LaRue
SPEEDWELL: Chief Boatswain Alfred B. Muse.
VIOLET: Chief Boatswain John M. Kendley.
WINNISIMMET: Boatswain Ottar Skotheim.

NARCISSUS: Boatswain Charles R. Cummings.
WISTARIA: Boatswain Linwood Hudgins.
MISTLETOW: Boatswain Eddie B. Mason.
LINDEN: Boatswain Gustav Nord.
ORCHID
CGC 2, 21, 26, 41, 43, 45.
CGC 128, 140, 143, 218, 288, 440, 441.

LIGHTSHIPS

NO. 115—FRYING PAN SHOALS: Boatswain Karl J. Torstersen.
NO. 91—RELIEF: Boatswain Cladius C. Austin.

NO. 107—WINTER QUARTER: Boatswain Bernard W. Diggs.
NO. 116—CHESAPEAKE BAY.
NO. 105—DIAMOND SHOALS.

COAST GUARD STATIONS

Ocean City Station, Ocean City, Md.

Chief Boatswain Thomas T. Moore, commanding
Includes OCEAN CITY and North Beach Lifeboat Stations.

Chincoteague Station, Chincoteague Island, Va.

Chief Boatswain_____commanding
Includes Popes Island, ASSATEAGUE BEACH, and Wallops Beach Lifeboat Stations and Killick Shoal Light Station.

Wachapreague Station, Wachapreague, Va.

Includes Metomkin Inlet and PARRAMORE BEACH Lifeboat Stations.

Broadwater Station, Broadwater, Va.

Chief Boatswain_____commanding
Includes Little Machipongo Inlet, HOG ISLAND, and Cobb Island Lifeboat Station.

Townsend Station, Townsend, Va.

Includes SMITH ISLAND LIFEBOAT STATION and Cape Charles Light Station.

Virginia Beach Station, Virginia Beach, Va.

Chief Boatswain Truxton E. Midgett, commanding
Includes Little Creek, VIRGINIA BEACH, and Little Island Lifeboat Stations and Cape Henry Light Station.

Kill Devil Hills Station, Kill Devil Hills, N. C.

Chief Boatswain_____commanding
Includes Caffeys Inlet, KILL DEVIL HILLS and Nags Head Lifeboat Stations and Bodie Island Light Station.

Rodanthe Station, Rodanthe, N. C.

Chief Boatswain_____commanding
Includes Oregon Inlet, Pea Island, and CHICAMACOMICO Lifeboat Stations and Roanoke Marshes Light Station.

Buxton Station, Buxton, N. C.

Includes Big Kinnakeet and CAPE HATTERAS Lifeboat Stations.

Ocracoke Station, Ocracoke, N. C

Includes Hatteras Inlet and OCRACOKE Lifeboat stations and Ocracoke Light Station.

Beaufort Station, Beaufort, N. C.

Includes Cape Lookout and FORT MACON Lifeboat Stations and Cape Lookout Light Station.

Southport Station, Southport, N. C.

Includes OAK ISLAND LIFEBOAT STATION and Cape Fear Light Station.

LIFEBOAT STATIONS

Wash Woods Lifeboat Station, Corolla, N. C.
Atlantic Lifeboat Station, Atlantic, N. C.

Swansboro Lifeboat Station, Swansboro, N. C.

Page from the *Register Of The Commissioned and Warrant Officers and Cadets, And Ships And Stations Of The United States Coast Guard*, 1 JUL 40, (U.S. Coast Guard)

Surfmen, winter uniform, possibly Fire Island LBSTA in New York, ca. 1923. Man on front row, far left is Earl Willis and next to him is Edgar O'Neal, both from Hatteras, NC. Note uniform and shoe style and the surfman devices on hats and collars. (Dalton Burrus)

Surfman's medals. Left to right: American Defense, Coast Guard Good Conduct, WW II Victory. Note bars on GCM inscribed with group name (awarded for service at Kill Devil Hills LBSTA). When a Coast Guardsman shipped over, a bar denoting cutter or station was awarded. Not shown are CG Expert Pistol and Rifle, American Campaign, and National Defense Medals for this surfmen. (Sheldon O'Neal and author)

Surfmen from Virginia and North Carolina, Engine School, Norfolk, 1930. Man on back row, third from right, is John E. Sterling, Metomkin Inlet LBSTA. Man on second row, second from right is Ben Wroten, Virginia Beach LBSTA. (John E. Sterling)

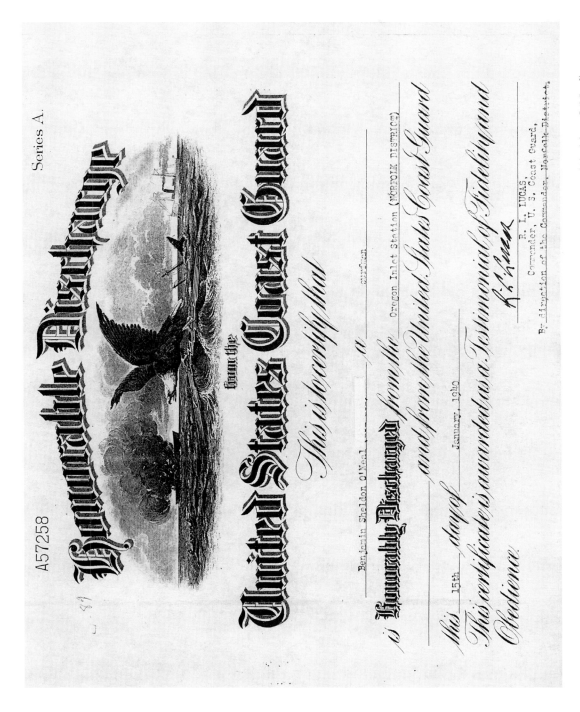

Surfman's discharge certificate, Oregon Inlet LBSTA, 15 JAN 40. Note ornate illustration. (Sheldon O'Neal)

OLD LIFEBOAT STATIONS

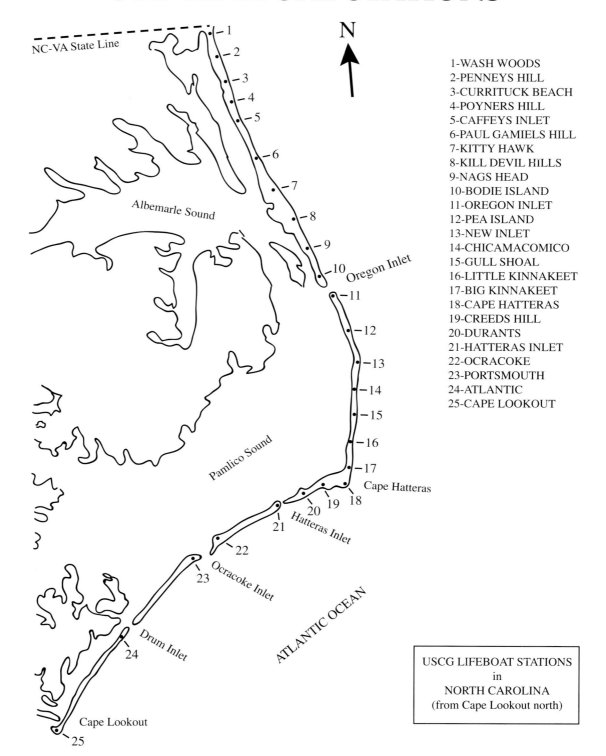

N

NC-VA State Line

1-WASH WOODS
2-PENNEYS HILL
3-CURRITUCK BEACH
4-POYNERS HILL
5-CAFFEYS INLET
6-PAUL GAMIELS HILL
7-KITTY HAWK
8-KILL DEVIL HILLS
9-NAGS HEAD
10-BODIE ISLAND
11-OREGON INLET
12-PEA ISLAND
13-NEW INLET
14-CHICAMACOMICO
15-GULL SHOAL
16-LITTLE KINNAKEET
17-BIG KINNAKEET
18-CAPE HATTERAS
19-CREEDS HILL
20-DURANTS
21-HATTERAS INLET
22-OCRACOKE
23-PORTSMOUTH
24-ATLANTIC
25-CAPE LOOKOUT

Albemarle Sound

Pamlico Sound

Oregon Inlet

Cape Hatteras

Hatteras Inlet

Ocracoke Inlet

ATLANTIC OCEAN

Drum Inlet

Cape Lookout

USCG LIFEBOAT STATIONS
in
NORTH CAROLINA
(from Cape Lookout north)

(Map, station locations, Wash Woods to Cape Lookout)

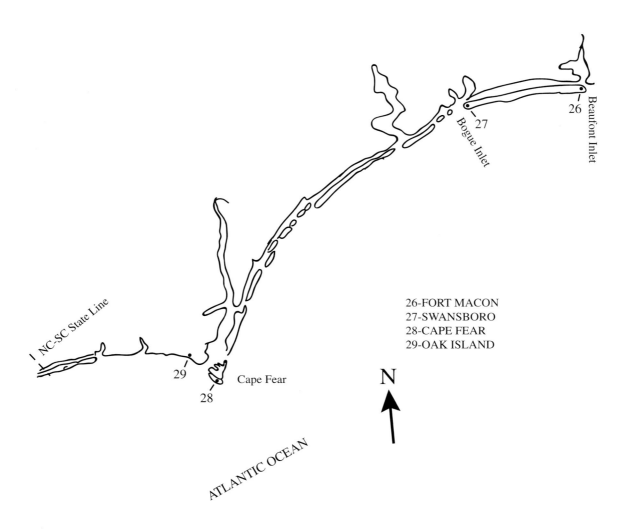

26-FORT MACON
27-SWANSBORO
28-CAPE FEAR
29-OAK ISLAND

N

USCG LIFEBOAT STATIONS
in
NORTH CAROLINA
(from Cape Fear north
to Beaufort Inlet)

(Map, station locations, Fort Macon to Oak Island)

Surfmen, Wash Woods LBSTA, ca. 1930. Front row, left to right: Boatswain (L) Augustus W. Styron (officer-in-charge), BM1c (L) Troy Morris, Raymond L. Williams, Willie A. Austin. Back row, left to right: James B. Beasley, Woodson Midgett, William T. Twiford, Ignatius Scarborough, Robert L. Austin. (Courtesy of The Mariners' Museum, Newport News, Va.)

WASH WOODS
1878-1951

This is the northern-most station in North Carolina. It was originally named "Deals Island." The original 1876-Type building was located almost on the state line. It was replaced in 1919 by a Chatham-Type building about two miles south of the original building. The second building, 7 3/8 miles north by west of the Currituck Beach Light, is now privately owned and still in fairly good condition. The station is accessible only from the south through Corolla by 4-wheel drive vehicle. The old station and lookout tower are clearly visible from the beach. The current owner rents it out.

Keeper Malachi Corbell from this station won the Gold Lifesaving Medal for rescuing two fishermen in 1878. This was the first such award in North Carolina.

Wash Woods LBSTA, 3 AUG 92. This is the northern-most station in North Carolina. At the time of this writing it is privately owned and is still in good condition. It is accessible from the south through Corolla by four-wheel drive vehicle. Note the short lookout tower. (author)

PENNYS HILL
1878-1937

This 1876-Type building was originally located 5 3/4 miles north of Currituck Beach Light. In 1948 it was moved down to Corolla and placed across from the boathouse of the Whalehead Club. In 1978 it was moved over to the oceanfront in front of the Currituck Beach station. In the mid-1980's it was moved back to its original location, and a few months later it burned. This station was originally named "Old Currituck Inlet."

Pennys Hill LBSTA, looking north, 29 APR 35. Surfmen and their families lived in the small buildings behind station. Built 1878, this building was moved to Corolla in the late 1940's. In the 1980's it was moved back to original site and shortly afterwards it burned. (National Park Service)

CURRITUCK BEACH
1874-ca.1937

The original 1874-Type station building was replaced in 1903 with a Quono-chontaug-Type building, located in Corolla about a mile north of Currituck Beach

Surfmen, Currituck Beach (Whales Head) LBSTA, ca. 1930. Left to right: CBM (L) Peter T. Henley (officer-in-charge), BM1c (L) Caleb C. Bowden, BM1c (L) Samuel B. Beasley, Earlie Midgett, Lewis L. Lewark, Jennings B. Sanderlin, Sammie E. Beasley, Jesse J. Johnson. Of all the old stations north of Caffey's Inlet LBSTA, this is the only one still in existence at the time of this writing. (Courtesy of The Mariner's Museum, Newport News, Va.)

Light. Its original name was "Jones Hill." Later on it was also known as "Whales Head." The original building was moved to a site just west of the 1903 building and was torn down in 1959. In the mid-1980's the 1903 building was moved approximately six miles north and placed on a site about 1,000 feet west of the original Pennys Hill station site. It is now a private residence and is still in good condition. Sand dunes have drifted up next to it in places. It is accessible only by 4- wheel drive vehicle from the south through Corolla. It sits well back off the beach behind the dune line and is clearly visible from the beach.

Currituck Beach LBSTA, 2 OCT 99. (author)

POYNERS HILL
1878-1937

The original 1876-Type station building and the Chicamacomico-Type station building, built in 1913, were located 5 1/2 miles south southeast of Currituck Beach Light. The original building was moved to Corolla in 1949. In 1975 it was moved again a few yards north to an oceanfront lot. In 1988 it was struck by light-

Poyners Hill LBSTA (in center), Corolla, ca. 1949. Ray T. Adams bought the Whalehead Club in 1940, and he moved this station and others here to Corolla in the late 1940's and early 1950's. All buildings in picture no longer exist. (Outer Banks History Center)

ning and burned. The 1913 building was not moved, and it also burned accidentally (1979). Today only the foundation of the second station plus the foundation of a WW II barracks building remain.

Poyners Hill LBSTA, 24 SEP 53. This second station, built in 1913 and closed in 1937, burned in 1979. (Courtesy of The Mariners' Museum, Newport News, Va.)

CAFFEYS INLET
1874-1964

The 1874-Type building was replaced in 1897 by a Quonochontaug-Type building which is now the restaurant at The Sanderling Inn Resort and Conference Center. It is located a short distance north of Duck. The station building is in excellent condition and contains interesting displays of Life-Saving Service and Coast Guard photographs and memorabilia, including a Lyle gun.

Surfmen, Caffey's Inlet LBSTA, ca. 1930's. Left to right: Boatswain (L) Truxton E. Midgett (officer-in-charge), BM1c (L) Aubrey Harris, BM1c (L) Willouby Olds, Walter Beacham, Doc Fulcher, Melvin Tillett. (Courtesy of The Mariners' Museum, Newport News, Va.)

Caffeys Inlet LBSTA, March 1962. Aftermath of the Ash Wednesday Storm, a terrible northeaster that struck the Outer Banks. This site is now occupied by The Sanderling Inn and Conference Center. Station building is now a restaurant. (Courtesy of The Mariners' Museum, Newport News, Va.)

PAUL GAMIELS HILL
1878-1937

The 1876-Type station building was located near Duck, 5 miles north of Kitty Hawk. It was a private residence after decommissioning, and it burned in the early 1960's.

Surfmen, Paul Gamiels Hill LBSTA, ca. 1930. Left to right: Boatswain (L) G. G. Snow (officer-in-charge), BM1c (L) E. A. Simmons, BM1c (L) A. D. Tillett, R. L. Wescott, J. L. Beacham, Manie Haywood, C. C. Dowdy, D. O. Scarborough, T. S. Midgett. (Courtesy of The Mariners' Museum, Newport News, Va.)

Paul Gamiels Hill LBSTA, ca. 1950. Closed in 1937, it burned in early 1960's. Note wreck pole in left foreground. (Courtesy of The Mariners' Museum, Newport News, Va.)

KITTY HAWK
1874-1937

At the time of this writing the 1874-Type station building is still in Kitty Hawk and is part of the Black Pelican Restaurant. It has been considerably modified and added to, but the original features of the front of the old station are still visible.

Kitty Hawk Lifesaving Station, 1983. This station was built in 1874 and is now part of the Black Pelican Restaurant in Kitty Hawk. Even though extensive additions have been made to the original structure the unmistakable original roof remains basically unchanged. (author)

Kitty Hawk LBSTA, 1983. This second station building had it foundation threatened by a severe northeaster in 1983 and was moved across Beach Road as a result. At the time of this writing it is still there, near milepost 4 1/2, and is a private residence. (author)

The Chicamacomico-Type station which was built in 1911 is still in good condition and is now a private residence. It was originally located on the ocean side of Beach Road but had to be moved to the present location on the west side of the road due to shoreline migration in the early 1980's. It is near Mile Post 4½ on Beach Road.

Kitty Hawk LBSTA, view looking north, ca. 1930. In early 1980's shoreline migration threatened builiding, and it was moved to west side of Beach Road. At the time of this writing this is a private residence. (Courtesy of The Mariners' Museum, Newport News, Va.)

KILL DEVIL HILLS
1878-1964

The original 1876-Type building is now privately owned. It was purchased by Doug Twiddy and moved to Corolla in 1986 where it is now a gift shop. The second station building (Southern Pattern-Type) is located on Beach Road near Mile Post 8 1/2 . When the Coast Guard closed the station the property reverted to the original family owners, and the station has been a private residence ever since. It is still in good condition.

DUKW (amphibious truck) entering surf, Kill Devil Hills LBSTA, 1943. (National Archives)

Kill Devil Hills LBSTA, view looking west, 1951. Note 1878 building at lower left, wreck pole in center, station number panel by tower, and isolation of site. (National Archives)

DUKW (amphibious truck) from Kill Devil Hills LBSTA at Croatan Inn, Beach Road, Milepost 7 1/2, Kill Devil Hills, ca. 1950. Croatan Inn closed years ago. Building in right background has been torn down, building at left is Quagmires Restaurant at the time of this writing. (Outer Banks History Center)

Aftermath of Ash Wednesday Storm, Kill Devil Hills LBSTA, 8 MAR 62. Note flooding along beach road as a result of overwash caused by tidal surge. (National Archives)

DUKW and 26-foot pulling boat, Kill Devil Hills LBSTA, 1943. A DUKW is an amphibious 6×6 truck developed by General Motors early in WW II . They were in service in the Coast Guard until the early 1960's. (National Archives)

Nags Head LBSTA, 1954. House at far left on beach was residence of Paul Midgett, officer-in-charge. This site is near the present location of Town of Nags Head water tower. (National Archives)

NAGS HEAD
1874-1957

Both the original station building and the Chicamacomico-Type station built in 1912 are no longer in existence. The station was severely damaged in March of 1962 during the Ash Wednesday Storm. At that time it was an Army air defense radar station. The station was located on the ocean side of Beach Road near the present day Nags Head town hall and water tower.

A surfman at this station, MoMM1c (L) Thomas E. Dough, won the Silver Lifesaving Medal in 1944.

Presentation of Silver Lifesaving Medal, 23 OCT 44. Left to right: CAPT Norman C. Manyon, MoMM 1c (L) Thomas E. Dough, LT Charles O. Peel . Motor Machinist's Mate Dough, from Manteo, enlisted in 1926 and served at Oregon Inlet LBSTA before WW II. During the war he was engineer on a landing craft in the invasion of North Africa in 1942 and was later sent to New Caledonia in the Pacific. When he returned from overseas he was assigned to Nags Head LBSTA. He won the medal there on 4 JUL 44 when he swam out 150 yards through a strong tide and surf too rough to launch a boat to assist a swimmer suffering a heart attack. Twice before, at Oregon Inlet in 1940 and later in New York, he swam to the assistance of someone in distress. His father Thomas A. Dough served for 33 years in the Life-Saving Service and Coast Guard. (Outer Banks History Center)

Former Nags Head LBSTA, March, 1962. Aftermath of Ash Wednesday Storm, a terrible north-easter that hit the Outer Banks on the 6th and 7th of March 1962. Note building damage and Army sign. Site is near present day Town of Nags Head water tower. (Outer Banks History Center)

DUKW (amphibious truck), Nags Head LBSTA, 23 JUL 53. Note propeller and rudder under stern. (National Park Service)

Nags Head LBSTA 26-foot pulling boat and crew, 1949. Left to right: BMC (L) Paul Midgett (officer- in-charge), EN1 (L) Thomas E. Dough, Howard Jones, David Farrow, Sidney Toler, Edgar Midgett, Earl Midgett, Alston Meekins, and Ira Peel. All were from either Manteo, Kitty Hawk or Avon. (National Archives)

Nags Head LBSTA boat crew preparing to launch into surf, 1949. (National Archives)

DUKW (amphibious truck), somewhere along the Outer Banks, ca. 1950. They were in service at Caffeys Inlet, Kill Devil Hills, Nags Head, Chicamacomico, Oregon Inlet, Cape Hatteras, and Fort Macon LBSTA's in 1940's-1960's. (Outer Banks History Center)

26-foot pulling boat and DUKW, Nags Head LBSTA, 2 May 49. BMC (L) Paul Midgett, officer-in-charge, is standing in the boat. (National Archives)

Beach apparatus drill, Nags Head LBSTA, 2 MAY 49. BMC (L) Paul Midgett is standing over Lyle gun and EN1 (L) Thomas E. Dough is to his immediate right.(National Archives)

BODIE ISLAND
1878-ca 1937

Both the 1876-Type station building and the Chatham-Type building built in 1925 are now owned and used by the National Park Service. They are in good condition and located about a mile north of Bodie Island Light. This station's original name was "Tommy's Hummock." While the new Oregon Inlet station was being built in the late 1980's the Oregon Inlet crew temporarily lived in the 1925 building.

Bodie Island LBSTA, 18 JUL 17. Built in 1878, this old station is about a mile north of Bodie Island Light. At the time of this writing this building is owned by the National Park Service and is in good condition. (Outer Banks History Center)

Bodie Island LBSTA, 3 OCT 98. This was second building at this site. Used temporarily in 1988 while new Oregon Inlet station was being built, it is owned by National Park Service. (author)

OREGON INLET
1874

This station's original name was "Bodie Island." The 1874-Type building was replaced in 1898 by a Quonochontaug-Type building. This building is located at the northern end of Pea Island near the bridge approach. It was abandoned by the Coast Guard in November of 1988 due to shoreline migration. At the time of this

26-foot MSB from Oregon Inlet LBSTA, 24 APR 42. Left to right:?, Chesley Midgett, Hurbert Midgett. (Sheldon O'Neal)

Oregon Inlet LBSTA, ca. 1956. Note wreck pole at left. Built in 1898, this building was vacated by the Coast Guard in November of 1988. At the time of this writing it is deteriorating. (U.S. Coast Guard Historian's Office Photo)

writing it is owned by Dare County and is slowly deteriorating from vandalism and the elements. Sand is drifting onto the site as the dunes in front of it slowly move back. In the late 1980's a new small boat SAR station was built across the inlet on the southern end of Bodie Island near the marina.

38-foot cabin picket boats, President's Cup Regatta, Potomac River, Washington, D.C., September 1949. Oregon Inlet LBSTA boat thought to be second from left. Note Washington Monument in background. (Outer Banks History Center)

Nora (station mascot) and CBM (L) Thomas J. "Jep" Harris, Officer-in-Charge, Oregon Inlet LBSTA, 1 DEC 43. Posed reenactment. The previous month Nora had found one of the men from the station who had fainted out along the cold, windswept beach while on patrol. She picked up his hat and ran back to the station with it to alert them to his danger. Thanks to Nora's quick thinking the seaman, Evans E. Mitchell from Chicago, was picked up and taken to the hospital where he recovered fully. Without Nora's help, he could have died from exposure. (Sheldon O'Neal)

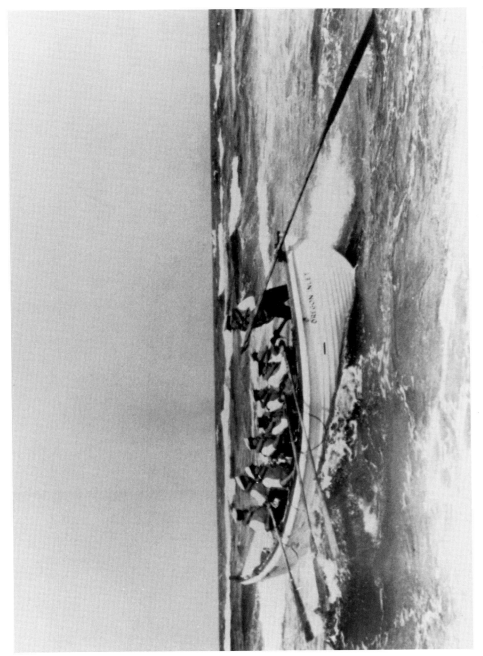

26-foot pulling boat from Oregon Inlet LBSTA, 24 JUN 46. CBM (L) Levene Midgett is coxswain standing in the stern at the sweep oar. Crew are all surfmen (note hat style) (Outer Banks History Center)

Oregon Inlet LBSTA, north end of Pea Island, looking north, 27 AUG 45. Note distance between station and inlet at top right. Also note remnant of long pier from station site angling up and out to left. (National Park Service)

PEA ISLAND
1878-1947

The 1876-Type building was located opposite what is now Pea Island National Wildlife Refuge headquarters on Pea Island. The first building burned mysteriously and was replaced in the early 1880's (1882-Type building?). A third building replaced the 1880's building sometime after 1915. After the station was closed the third building was moved down to the village of Salvo where it is now a private residence. A cistern and the lookout tower were also moved with the station building.

Pea Island LBSTA, looking west, 3 JAN 35. Building was moved to Salvo after station closed, and, at the time of this writing, it is a private residence. CBM (L) Maxi Berry was the last officer-in-charge here. (National Park Service)

Aftermath of Ash Wednesday Storm, Pea Island LBSTA, 8 MAR 62. Note damage to dunes and how close station is to ocean compared to earlier photograph. Highway pictured here is now covered by dunes, and new highway is farther west. (National Park Service)

Pea Island Lifesaving Station Gold Lifesaving Medal display, North Carolina Aquarium, Manteo. Medal awarded posthumously in 1996 to the black keeper and surfmen of this station for a rescue in 1896. (author)

This was the only station in the Life-Saving Service and Coast Guard manned by an all black crew. A plaque at the North Carolina Aquarium in Manteo commemorates this station. Keeper Richard Etheridge and Surfmen Benjamin Bowser, Lewis Wescott, Dorman Pugh, Theodore Meekins, Stanley Wise, and William Irving from this station rescued nine people off of the schooner *E.S. Newman* in 1896. In 1996, on the one hundredth anniversary of that brave deed, this station was posthumously awarded a Gold Lifesaving Medal. At the time of this writing the medal and citation are on display at the aquarium in Manteo, and a second set is on display in the entrance foyer of the Park Service office in Manteo.

Surfmen and 26-foot pulling boat, Pea Island LBSTA, ca. 1940. Beach wagon's front axle was unhooked at water's edge in order to move boat off wagon for launching. (Outer Banks History Center)

NEW INLET
1882-1916

This station (1882-Type) was located 3 miles south of New Inlet near the village of Rodanthe. Sometime after it closed it burned and was never rebuilt. In the early part of this century storm overwash caused serious erosion around this station which made its continued operation difficult. Consequently, this station was closed, and the Pea Island station was moved to compensate.

New Inlet LBSTA, 13 JUL 16. Built in 1882, this station was closed the year this picture was taken. It later burned. (National Park Service)

Chicamacomico LBSTA, 1951. Note DUKW (amphibious truck) parked to the left of station and the station number 179 sign at far right beside flag pole. This station, now a museum, is the most complete and best preserved of all the old stations on the North Carolina coast. (National Archives)

CHICAMACOMICO
1874-1954

The original 1874-Type and the 1911 Chicamacomico-Type buildings as well as the kitchen building and all other outbuildings are still at the original station site in the village of Rodanthe. They have been restored by the Chicamacomico Historical Association. The station is now a museum with USLSS and USCG uniforms, caps, pictures, and other memorabilia on display. This station complex is one of the best preserved and most complete in the country. Once a week in the summertime Park Service rangers and volunteers put on a beach apparatus drill reenactment for visitors.

The famous *Mirlo* rescue in 1918 was carried out by the keeper and surfmen from this station. The 26-foot motor surfboat used in the *Mirlo* rescue has been restored and is on display in the 1874 building which is also being restored. The following men received Gold Lifesaving Medals and Grand Crosses of the American Cross of Honor for this daring rescue:

Arthur V. Midgett
Clarence E. Midgett
John Allen Midgett Jr.
Leroy S. Midgett
Zion S. Midgett
Prochorus L. O'Neal

Surfmen, Gull Shoal LBSTA, ca. 1930. Left to right: CBM (L) Palmer Midgett, BM1c (L) Leroy Midgett, Surfman Clarence Midgett, Surfman Graves Midgett. Leroy and Clarence Midgett won Gold Lifesaving Medals for the *Mirlo* rescue in 1918 when they were at Chicamacomico LBSTA. (National Park Service)

GULL SHOAL
1878-1937

The 1876-Type station building was destroyed in the 1944 hurricane. This station was once called "Cedar Hummock," and it was located 11 3/4 miles south of New Inlet near the present day Salvo campground.

Rasmus S. Midgett, a surfman at this station, single-handedly rescued ten people from the grounded barkentine *Priscilla* in 1899 and was awarded the Gold Life-saving Medal for so bravely risking his life to save others. The surfman made ten trips out to the ship on his faithful horse, Gilbert, and each time he returned to shore with another person. He also rode back out three more times to retrieve the bodies of those who didn't survive.

Gull Shoal LBSTA, 15 JUL 17. Note galley at left. Built 1878, station washed down in the 1944 hurricane. Site is near the present Salvo campground. (National Park Service)

Little Kinnakeet LBSTA, view looking west, 1954. This property, including the original station building in center, is undergoing restoration by National Park Service at the time of this writing. (National Archives)

LITTLE KINNAKEET
1874-1938
ca.1945-1954

Both the original 1874-Type lifesaving station building and the 1904 Southern Pattern-Type building are in fair condition. This station is located 5 1/2 miles north of Cape Hatteras Light, north of Avon village. The National Park Service owns the buildings now and is in the process of restoring them at the time of this writing.

BIG KINNAKEET
1878-ca. 1946

Both the 1876-Type lifesaving station building and the Chatham-Type station built in 1929 were damaged in the 1944 hurricane and demolished later. They were located 1 1/2 miles north of Cape Hatteras Light, south of Avon village, near Askins Creek. At the time of this writing, other than a concrete slab and bits of debris, all traces of this old station are gone.

Big Kinnakeet LBSTA, 10 NOV 34. Note station number 182 on roof (for identification by aircraft). Built in 1929, this was second station building at this site south of Avon. Damaged in the 1944 hurricane, it was eventually torn down. (National Park Service)

Cape Hatteras Lifesaving Station, ca. 1900. Built in 1882 1 3/8 mile south of Cape Hatteras Light—in service until ca.1940 when replaced by a new station building—torn down ca. 1948 when a Coast Guard Loran station was built on this site. Left to right: Urias Williams, Edward Midgett, Baxter Miller, John Howard Midgett, Issac Jennette, Ed Stowe, Dave Barnett, Captain Pat Etheridge (Keeper), and their dog Rover. The two men standing on the porch are, left to right, Dr. Josh J. Davis and Theodore Meekins. Man in white at right rear of Etheridge is Charlie Olsen, the cook. (Dalton Burrus)

CAPE HATTERAS
1882

Located one mile south of Cape Hatteras Light near Cape Point, the 1882-Type lifesaving station was demolished in 1948 when a Loran station was built on the site. In 1939-40 a second LBSTA building was built a short distance to the west of it. The second building also housed Group Cape Hatteras in addition to the LBSTA crew. Use of boats and the LBSTA function here were phased out sometime between 1951 and 1966, after which time only the group operation continued. Group Cape Hatteras moved into the former Navy installation a short distance north of Cape Hatteras Light in 1985, and at the time of this writing it is still in operation there. The National Park Service now owns and uses the 1939 station and equipment buildings. A small British cemetery is near this station.

Ben Dixon MacNeill, well known North Carolina newspaperman and author, lived in a small house near here when he retired in 1945 until his death in 1960. He

Surfmen, Cape Hatteras LBSTA, July 1921. Man in back row, second from left, is Loran Barnett. (Outer Banks History Center)

Site of first Cape Hatteras station and Loran station, 16 FEB 2000. Cape Hatteras Light stands outside of view, to the left. Ocean is beyond dune in background. (author)

was a frequent visitor at this station and had Sunday dinner here with the crew many times. He was well liked by George Meekins, the group commander, and his men; and he, in turn, thought a lot of them. He wrote about this station and the crew in his books, *The Hatterasman* and *Sand Roots*.

Gold Lifesaving Medals were awarded to Keeper Benjamin B. Dailey and Surfmen Issac L. Jennett, Thomas Gray, John H. Midgett, Jabez B. Jennett, and Charles E. Fulcher of this station for rescuing nine men from the foundering barkentine *Ephraim Williams* five miles offshore in 1885. The Gold Lifesaving Medal was awarded to Surfman (acting Keeper) Baxter B. Miller from this station for the 1909 *Brewster* rescue on the Outer Diamonds off Cape Hatteras. Silver Lifesaving Medals were awarded to Surfmen H. S. Miller, O. O. Midgett, I. L. Jennett, E. J. Midgett, U. B. Williams, and W. L. Barnett from this station for the 1909 *Brewster* rescue. In 1911 the Silver Lifesaving Medal was awarded to Surfman Baxter B. Miller from this station for saving John H. Dailey (son of Captain B. B. Dailey) who was swept overboard in heavy weather. Years later other surfmen from this station won four Silver Lifesaving Medals for the 1931 *Anna May* rescue on Outer Diamonds off Cape Hatteras.

Cape Hatteras LBSTA, looking west, 22 MAY 35. This building (built 1882) was replaced by a second station building 1939-40. In 1948 a Loran station was built at this site, and this building was torn down. Nothing remains at this site. (Outer Banks History Center)

Cape Hatteras LBSTA, 1954. This second station at Cape Hatteras was built in 1939-40. The first station and the Loran station were closer to the beach, off to the right of this picture. Note the most famous lighthouse in America near top. The Park Service took over this site when the Coast Guard moved out in 1985, and, at the time of this writing, they still use the telephone, main station, and equipment buildings. Towers, wreck pole, and small buildings were taken down and removed years ago. (National Archives)

Creeds Hill LBSTA, March, 1930. Built 1918, this was second station at this site. It was moved west of Frisco beside Route 12 (about two miles west of its original site). At the time of this writing it is a private residence. (Courtesy of The Mariners' Museum, Newport News, VA.)

CREEDS HILL
1878-1937

The 1876-Type lifesaving station building and the Chatham-Type station built in 1918 were once located 4 miles SW of Cape Hatteras Lighthouse. Now the 1918 building is a private residence. It was moved west of Frisco village on Route 12, about 2 miles west of its original site.

The Gold Lifesaving Medal was awarded to Keeper Patrick H. Etheridge at this station for assisting the Cape Hatteras station crew in the 1885 *Ephraim Williams* rescue. Keeper Eugene H. Peel from this station received the Gold Lifesaving Medal and Surfmen D. E. Fulcher, V. O. Gaskins and W. H. Austin received the Silver Lifesaving Medal for the rescue of 28 men from the German steamer *Brewster* that foundered on the Outer Diamonds off Cape Hatteras in 1909.

DURANTS
1878 - ca. 1937

The 1876-Type building is 3 miles east of Hatteras Inlet on Route 12. Its original name was "Hatteras." At the time of this writing It is privately owned and part of a motel complex named "Durants Station."

Durants LBSTA, looking east, 12 JUL 17. Built in 1878, this station building, at the time of this writing, is part of Durants Station, a motel complex. (Outer Banks History Center)

Durants LBSTA, 16 FEB 2000. Part of motel, "Durants Station," at the time of this writing. (author)

Beach apparatus drill, somewhere on the Outer Banks (possibly Durants LBSTA), ca. 1920. Drill was performed weekly at all Life-Saving Service stations from the 1870's up to 1915 and afterwards at Coast Guard stations until the early 1960's, when it was phased out. (Outer Banks History Center)

Hatteras Inlet LBSTA. north end of Ocracoke Island, looking south, 1949. This was the second Hatteras Inlet station (built 1917). The inlet is out of view at bottom of picture. (National Archives)

Hatteras Inlet LBSTA, north end of Ocracoke Island, looking south, 1955. Sea has claimed the station building and pier. Boathouse burned in the summer of 1950. Note extensive shoreline migration compared to 1949 picture. (National Archives)

Hatteras Inlet LBSTA, 8 NOV 55. Built 1917 on north end of Ocracoke Island, sea has finally claimed it after years of extensive shoreline migration. No trace of this building remains (only pilings offshore). (Courtesy of the Mariners' Museum, Newport News, Va.)

Hatteras Inlet LBSTA, 20 NOV 61. This was the third Hatteras Inlet station. It was in service from 1954 until 1963. This was originally the Gooseville hunt club, and it is near the present day ferry docks and Station Hatteras Inlet (fourth station, opened in 1963). (National Park Service).

Crew, Hatteras Inlet LBSTA (Gooseville hunt club site), ca. 1955. Left to right: (1st row) BMC Edward Midgett (officer-in-charge), BM1 Clayton Brothers, EN1 Preston Quidley, CS2 Jackie Willis (cook); (2nd row) BM2 Basil Hooper, BM1 Edward Scarborough, BM3 Wesley Gray, SN Edward Austin, SN Gearhart; (3rd row) SN Ernest Styron, SN Robbins, SN Buchanan, SN Donald Austin, SN Leon Jennette, EN3 Johnny Williams. (Johnny Williams)

HATTERAS INLET
1882

Over the years there have been four locations for this station. The first life-saving station (1882/1883-Type building) was on the north end of Ocracoke Island, and it washed down from shoreline migration. It was originally named "Ocracoke."

The second (1917) station was a Chatham-Type building, and it was also located on the north end of Ocracoke Island. On July 14, 1950, the station boathouse (built in 1940) burned and was never rebuilt. In November of 1955 the station washed down after years of shoreline migration. A few pilings offshore are all that remains of the 1917 station on Ocracoke. In December of 1931 CBM (L) Levene Midgett was the officer-in-charge of this station, and he and surfmen from this station won Silver Lifesaving Medals for the *Anna May* rescue on the Outer Diamonds off Cape Hatteras.

In the early 1950's the Coast Guard purchased the Gooseville hunt club property across the inlet on Hatteras Island. The station was at this site from the mid-1950's until the early 1960's when it was again relocated, this time to a modern two story brick station near the ferry dock. Station Hatteras Inlet is still operational at the time of this writing.

OCRACOKE
1904

The original Southern Pattern-Type station building on Silver Lake in the village of Ocracoke was torn down in the 1940's. A new station, boathouse and launchways, and equipment building were built at the same site in 1939-40 just before WW II. The original station site was behind the 1940 building. Ocracoke became a sub-station under Station Hatteras Inlet in 1995-96, and the crew moved to smaller quarters nearby. However, the old station dock is still used by the Coast Guard. At the time of this writing the Coast Guard is considering reoccupying the 1940 building contingent upon appropriation of funding needed for modernization and renovation.

Ocracoke LBSTA (second station, built 1939-40), ca. 1942. Boats, left to right: 26-foot MSB, 36-foot MLB, 38-foot cabin picket boat. Note shallows in foreground. (Theodore Mutro)

Ocracoke LBSTA, under construction, December 1939. Note first station (built 1905) in background. The 1905 building was torn down sometime in the 1940's. (National Park Service)

Ocracoke LBSTA, 1954. Note equipment building to left of station, and Jeep parked behind station. 83-foot patrol boat, 38-foot cabin picket boat, and 45-foot buoy boat are moored at the pier. (National Archives)

PORTSMOUTH
1894 -1937

The Quonochontaug-Type lifesaving station building is in Portsmouth Village, a deserted community maintained by the National Park Service on Portsmouth Island. It can be reached by boat from nearby Ocracoke. The building is in very good condition.

Portsmouth LBSTA, summer of 1998. This building on Portsmouth Island, owned by the National Park Service, is open to visitors. It closed in 1937 and was used temporarily in WW II (1942-ca.1944) by Coast Guard Beach Patrol. (Jack Huber)

ATLANTIC
1895 -1965

Atlantic Lifeboat Station was a Quonochontaug-Type building located on Core Bank, an island which is part of Cape Lookout National Seashore. Shortly after it was closed by the Coast Guard the station burned. This station was originally named "Core Bank."

Atlantic LBSTA, 1952. Note 36-foot motor lifeboat moored at end of pier. This station was on Core Bank near Drum Inlet. It was closed in 1965 and later burned. (National Archives)

CAPE LOOKOUT
1887 -1982

This lifeboat station is located one and one half miles south of Cape Lookout Light and is in the Cape Lookout National Seashore administered by the National Park Service. The 1882-Type building was replaced by a Chatham–type building in 1916, and that second building is now used by the North Carolina Maritime Museum as a center for marine biology and related studies by school groups.

Keeper William H. Gaskill and Surfmen Kilby Guthrie, Walter M. Yeomans, Tyre Moore, John A. Guthrie, James W. Fulcher, John E. Kirkman, Calupt T. Jarvis, and Joseph L. Lewis (volunteer and former surfman) of this station were awarded Gold Lifesaving Medals for rescuing six men off the schooner *Sarah D. J. Rawson* in 1905. The rescuers were at sea for 28 hours.

Surfmen, Cape Lookout LBSTA, ca. 1930. Man second from left in front row is Jimmie Lewis from Marshallburg. Man in back row on the left is Luther Guthrie from Harkers Island. (U.S. Coast Guard Historian's Office Photo)

36-foot motor lifeboat (MLB), Cape Lookout LBSTA, ca. 1930. This type boat (self-righting and self-bailing) was replaced by the 44-foot MLB, beginning in 1963. The last one was taken out of service in 1987. (U.S. Coast Guard Historian's Office Photo)

Cape Lookout LBSTA, 1961. Left to right: main building (built 1916), galley, recreation room, equipment building (built 1939-40). (U.S. Coast Guard Historian's Office Photo)

FORT MACON
1904

The first station was a Southern Pattern-Type building located at Atlantic Beach, near the fort at Beaufort Inlet. The second 1936 type station building, boathouse with launchways, and equipment building were built in 1938. These two station buildings were torn down and replaced with a modern structure in 1965, but the boathouse and equipment building are still in service here. In addition to the small boat SAR station, Group Fort Macon, an Aids to Navigation Team, and a cutter base are in operation here also at the time of this writing.

Boat basin, view west from tower, Fort Macon LBSTA, 13 AUG 35. Basin has been extensively widened and dredged out with new docks and bulkheads constructed in 1941, 1946-47, and 1964-65. At the time of this writing this is home base for a 41-foot UTB, a 47-foot MLB, an 82-foot patrol boat, two 110-foot patrol boats, USCGC *Block Island*, USCGC *Staten Island*, USCGC *Elm*, and USCGC *Primrose*. (National Park Service)

Boathouse (built ca. 1940), Group Fort Macon, 15 FEB 2000. Note boathouse doors and launchways have been removed. Also note floating pier and 47-foot MLB. (author)

Boat basin, Fort Macon LBSTA, July 1934. Note surfmen's white summer uniforms, 26-foot pulling boat in foreground, 26-foot MSB behind it, 36-foot MLB on lift in background, and pile driver at far left. (National Park Service)

SWANSBORO
1904

The first station was a Southern Pattern-Type building, and its original name was "Bogue Inlet." It was replaced in the early 1940's with a 1936-type station and 3-bay boathouse and integral lookout tower (like the Ocracoke station building). It is located near the west end of Bogue Banks, on the inner shore, 1 1/2 miles east of Bogue Inlet. As of this writing it is now a sub-station under Station Fort Macon. The 1940's building is still in service; however, the launchways of the boat house have been removed, and the tower has been shortened. The equipment building is also still in service.

Boat basin, Swansboro LBSTA, ca. 1954. Note boat carriage and launchways. Left to right: 26-foot MSB and 30-foot rescue boat behind it, 36-foot MLB. (Dalton Burrus)

Swansboro LBSTA, 1954. Left to right: SN Donald T. Robinson, BMC Dalton Burrus (officer-in-charge), EN3 Jack Mason, ?, and mascot, Mickey (who wouldn't let strangers onto station grounds, he once chased two Marines off the site and out into the ocean). (Dalton Burrus)

Swansboro LBSTA, ca. 1955. Station was built in 1939-40, same plan as Ocracoke LBSTA. Launchways and upper level of tower have been removed, but station is still in service at time of this writing. (Dalton Burrus)

30-foot rescue boat from Swansboro LBSTA, ca. 1955. (Dalton Burrus)

Swansboro (Bogue Inlet) LBSTA, January 1938. This station was built in 1904 and was replaced in 1940 by a 1938 type building (still in service at the time of this writing). Note galley to right of main station building. (National Park Service)

CAPE FEAR
1881 -1937

The original 1882-Type station and the Chatham-Type station built in 1915 were located on Smith (Bald Head) Island. The Coast Guard temporarily reopened this station during WW II for use by the Beach Patrol. In the mid-1960's it accidentally burned. Today only a station boathouse converted into a private residence remains.

Cape Fear LBSTA, ca. 1916. This was the second station building on Bald Head Island. Built in 1915, it burned in the 1960's. (National Park Service)

OAK ISLAND
1888

This is the southern-most station in North Carolina, and it is located at Long Beach. The original 1882-Type station was moved across the road, diagonally across from the modern station. It is now a well maintained private residence. The second station building (Chatham-Type c.1930's) was demolished in the early 1990's when it was replaced by a new station building. This is still an active Coast Guard small boat station.

Oak Island Lifesaving Station, 1995. Built in 1888, this was the first station on Oak Island. Sometime after 1941 it was moved from its initial site across to the ocean side of the road. At the time of this writing it is a private residence, still in good condition, and it is one of the few remaining stations from this era in North Carolina. (author)

26-foot pulling boat capsize drill demonstration, Oak Island LBSTA crew, Fort Caswell (east end of Oak Island), midsummer of 1950. Spectators are Boy Scouts, scout officials, and parents. Bill Harris was coxswain and Howard Lockerman and Carl Yancey were in crew. (Howard Lockerman)

Oak Island LBSTA, 26 JUN 41. View from boat basin, looking south, left to right: first station building (1882-Type), second station building (Chatham-Type), equipment building (ca. 1939-40). Note boats on lifts and 36-foot MLB moored at pier in center. Before a channel was dredged through the marsh up to this station site sometime prior to July of 1934 the station's boats were moored out at the end of a 3,700 foot pier. (U.S. Coast Guard Historian's Office Photo)

A FEW OF THE MANY RESCUES AT NORTH CAROLINA STATIONS

MIRLO RESCUE – 1918

Boatswain (L) John Allen Midgett, Jr. was keeper of Chicamacomico Station from 1916 until 1937. He was the third of four keepers/officers-in-charge of that station, three of whom were named Midgett. The first was Bannister Midgett III, and Levene W. Midgett was the last officer in charge. In the summer of 1918, during World War I, a mine laid by the German U-boat *U-117* blew up the British tanker *Mirlo* within sight of Chicamacomico Station. The keeper and his crew of surfmen rescued the captain and crew of the burning vessel.

The following was excerpted from the station logbook for Friday, August 16, 1918, the day of that famous rescue.

4:00 p.m. to Mid. At 4:30 p.m. lookout reported seeing a great mass of water shoot up in the air which seemed to cover the after portion of a steamer that was about seven miles E by S of this Station and heading in a Northerly direction, a great quantity of smoke rising from the after part of the Steamer was noticed but continuing her course for a few minutes when she swung around for the beach and then heading off shore, the fire was now seen to shoot up from the stern of the Steamer and heavy explosions were heard. I called all hands including the liberty man and started with power Surfboat No. 1046. Wind N.E. moderate, heavy sea on beach, had difficulty in getting away from the beach, cleared the beach at about 5:00 p.m. and headed for the burning wreck, then about 5 miles off shore. I met one of the ship's boats with the captain and sixteen men in her; I was informed that their ship was a British tanker and that she was torpedoed [at the time a torpedo was suspected but later a mine was determined to be cause of blast] which caused the loss of ship. I was informed that two other boats were in the vicinity of the burning gas and oil that was coming up from the sunken ship. I directed the captain of that boat where and how to go and wait my arrival, but not to attempt a landing as the sea was strong and there was danger of him capsizing his boat without assistance. I then headed for the burning gas and oil. On arrival I found the sea a mass of wreckage and burning gas and oil, there were two great masses of flames about one hundred yards apart with the sea for many hundred yards in places covered with the burning gas. An in between the two great flames at times when the smoke would clear away a little, a life boat could be seen bottom up with six men clinging to it, the heavy swell washing over the boat. With great difficulty I ran our boat through the smoke, floating wreckage and burning gas and oil, and managed to rescue the six men from a burning sea. Who informed me that at times they had to dive under the water to save themselves from being burned to death, all had burns but non serious. They informed me that they were sure that there were no men afloat except those in the boats. But this did not stop our searching in the vicinity of the fire for those missing men, but no more men could be found. These six men seemed to know nothing of the other boats, they being lost sight of in the fire and great clouds of smoke that were rising from the burning gas and oil. I headed our boat before the sea and wind in hopes of finding the missing boat, and in a short time the 3RD which was the missing boat with nineteen men was sighted about nine miles S.E. of station. I ran alongside took this boat in tow and proceeded to where I had directed the first boat to be, this boat was soon reached and taken in tow. I had in station boat six men rescued from the bottom of overturned boat. And one of the boats being towed containing seventeen and the other boat containing nineteen, the wind was beginning to freshen from the N.E. and sea rising on beach. I was heading for my station when about two mile South of station it began to get dark and for safety I decided to make a landing. I anchored the two ship's boats about six hundred yards from the beach and transferred the men to station boat, landing all in station boat at four trips, and then put surfmen in the two ship's boats and had

Chicamacomico LBSTA pulling boat, 1918. Boatswain (L) John Allen Midgett Jr., coxswain standing in the stern, is ferrying the crew from the British tanker *Mirlo* out to a ship sent to pick them up. Captain Johnny, as his men called him, and his surfmen had recently rescued these men after their ship hit a mine and exploded and burned. (Outer Banks History Center)

them landed. As fast as the men were landed they were carried to the station by my team of horses and the horse from station No. 180 [Gull Shoal]. The Keeper and crew from station No. 180 met me at the beach and assisted me in landing the crew. All boats including the station boat were pulled up on the beach out of danger of the sea. I landed last trip at 9:00 p.m. and arrived at station at 11:00 p.m., myself and crew very tired. I furnished the Captain and all his crew who needed it medical aid, and then with some dry clothing, and their supper, and with a place to sleep. [signed John A. Midgett, Keeper]

After the war the British Board of Trade and the U. S. Coast Guard presented Captain Johnny (as his men called him) and his five surfmen with Gold Lifesaving Medals for gallantry and humanity in saving lives at sea. Those surfmen's names are:

Zion S. Midgett
Arthur V. Midgett
Clarence E. Midgett
Leroy S. Midgett
Prochorus L. O'Neal.

In July of 1930 Rear Admiral Frederick C. Billard, Commandant of the Coast Guard, presented all six men with Grand Crosses of the American Cross of Honor. Only eleven have ever been awarded. This rescue is surely one of the most daring and courageous in the annals of the Coast Guard.

Boatswain (L) John Allen Midgett Jr., ca. 1930. Enlisted USLSS 1896; keeper, Chicamacomico LBSTA 1916-1937; Mirlo rescue 16 AUG 18; awarded Gold Lifesaving Medal by the British government 8 NOV 18 (and silver cup by British Board of Trade); awarded Gold Lifesaving Medal by U.S. Coast Guard 20 AUG 24; awarded Grand Cross of the American Cross of Honor 30 JUL 30; died 1938. USCGC *Midgett* (WHEC-726), a Hamilton Class High Endurance Cutter named after him, was commissioned 17 MAR 72. (Outer Banks History Center)

Keeper and surfmen, Chicamacomico LBSTA, at Manteo, 30 JUL 30. RADM Frederick C. Billard, Commandant of the Coast Guard, (4th from right) has presented Boatswain (L) John Allen Midgett Jr. (3rd from right) and his surfmen Grand Crosses of the American Cross of Honor for their heroic rescue in 1918 of the crew of the British tanker, *Mirlo*. Surfmen present are Zion S. Midgett, Arthur V. Midgett, Prochorus O'Neal, Clarence E. Midgett, and Leroy Midgett. (Outer Banks History Center)

Kyzikes Rescue – 1927

During a strong northeaster in December of 1927 the Greek tank steamer *Kyzikes* was badly damaged and began taking on water approximately 200 miles off the Virginia Capes. A distress call was sent out around noon on Saturday, December 3. Other vessels that picked up the call were unable to render assistance, and the *Kyzikes* drifted helplessly before the storm while her crew fruitlessly tried to pump out the deeply laden vessel. In the process the tanker's fires went out and her engines stopped. She finally grounded off the beach at Kill Devil Hills at 4:35 Sunday morning. Later that morning former Coast Guardsman Joe Partridge, who lived at Kill Devil Hills, noticed the smell of oil. Thomas J. "Jep" Harris, a surfman from Kill Devil Hills Station, spotted the stricken ship while on the north patrol, Both men rushed to the station to alert the crew. Keeper Will H. Lewark immediately called the Kitty Hawk and Nags Head stations for assistance and proceeded to the wreck with his crew of surfmen and their beach apparatus. They had difficulty getting a line out to the ship. They finally managed to get the breeches buoy lines secured and brought all twenty-four of the men on the ship to shore. It was hard going from start to finish because the ship rolled so much that the lines were pulled high in the air and then dropped almost into the breakers. Surfman Will Dough wore the skin off his hands in the process, and the rescuers were nearly as exhausted as the rescued when the last man was hauled ashore at seven o'clock that night. Both CBM (L) Will H. Lewark, Officer-in-Charge of Kill Devil Hills Station, and CBM (L) Walter G. Etheridge, Officer-in-Charge of Nags Head Station, were promoted to Boatswain (L) for successfully directing the rescue.

ANNA MAY RESCUE - 1931

The following excerpts from the Hatteras Inlet LBSTA logbook for Wednesday and Thursday, 9 DEC 31 and 10 DEC 31 tell of another of the many daring rescues along the North Carolina coast.

[Wednesday]At 10:50 a.m. received telephone call from Officer in Charge, Cape Hatteras, and Creeds Hill Stations informing that they had been notified via Radio Station at Cape Hatteras that a small fishing steamer was grounded on Outer Diamonds Shoals and that they with their boats were leaving to investigate. At once called Ocracoke Station requested that Mo.M.M.1C(L) [Motor Machinist Mate 1st Class, Lifesaving Branch] Dallas Williams be immediately sent to this station to assist in getting Lifeboat motor in operating condition. The fresh South gale and rain with the high surf making it apparently impossible to any other

Surfmen, Kill Devil Hills LBSTA, ca. 1930. Third man from left is Thomas J. "Jep" Harris (enlisted as a surfman in 1925, retired as a chief boatswain's mate (L) in 1952, officer-in-charge of Oregon Inlet LBSTA during WW II). Officer-in-charge, at far left, may be Will H. Lewark. (Courtesy of The Mariner's Museum, Newport News, Va.)

boat available other than the Lifeboat to put to sea, out Hatteras Inlet...At 4:10 p.m. succeeded in getting Lifeboat motor started and proceeded to sea. Cleared bar and headed offshore approximately three miles, but due to high seas, strong South wind and rain and knowing that could not render any assistance during the night, and running great risk of losing both boat and crew if attempted to venture near the Diamond Shoals, decided best to return back to Inlet...

10 DEC 31:

Mid to 8:00 a.m. Cabin Picket Boat CG-2321 standing by for picket duty in harbor. BM1C(L) Willie H. Austin, in charge; Surfman Sumner M. Scarborough on board. At 4:00 a.m. Motor Lifeboat No. 3380, in command of C.B.M.(L) Levene W. Midgett; with Mo.M.M.1C(L) Dallas Williams [from the Ocracoke Station], Surfmen Richard Scarborough, Guy C. Quidley and Tommie G. Meekins on board; left in route to Diamond Shoals; cleared Hatteras Inlet Bar 4:50 a.m. Fresh breeze Southwest, Sea rough... Crew with Motor Lifeboat on arriving to the outer Diamond shoal found the fishing Steamer Anna May of Newport News Va. stranded and all submerged under water. The crew of five men all alive and lashed in the rigging. The vessel was rapidly breaking to pieces. Motor Surfboat from Cape Hatteras Station had previously arrived on the scene, was standing by, unable to render assistance by reason of the high breakers which was continuously sweeping the Steamer. Boatswain (L) B. R. Ballance advised that he had made several attempts to put line on board but unable to get near enough to reach the men in the rigging, and authorized that I use my judgment in any way I thought assistance could be given by Lifeboat. At once made attempt to run near and take the men out of the rigging with heaving lines, but owing to shallow water and high pounding breakers, was unable to do so. The second attempt was to run near the Steamer, put line over rigging with line throwing gun, anchor lifeboat, send ring buoy on board and take the men off, but before this could be brought in operation the mast with rigging and men was all swept away from the Steamer. The Lifeboat pounding heavy on the bottom made it impossible to get the men until they had been carried several yards in the ripraps by the current. Succeeded in getting three of the men, the other two were picked up by boat from Cape Hatteras. When the crew of five men had all been picked up both boats immediately headed for their Station... Crew with Lifeboat returned to Station with the shipwreck men 11:50 a.m. They were taken to the Station, given hot coffee, stripped and furnished clothing by Station crew, given light diet and put to bed.... At 6:30 p.m. the three shipwreck men was called for supper...All well recovered from their exposure and ate plentiful. They will be cared for at Station until convenient transportation is arranged....

[signed Levene W. Midgett, Officer in Charge]

On 17 DEC 35 Silver Lifesaving Medals were presented in Elizabeth City to the following Coast Guardsmen from the stations indicated for the *Anna May* rescue:

Boatswain (L) Bernice R. Ballance	Cape Hatteras
Surfman Baxter Jennett	Cape Hatteras
CBM (L) James M. Ketcham	Cape Hatteras
BM1c (L) Frank W. Miller	Cape Hatteras
Boatswain (L) John R. Austin	Big Kinnakeet
CBM (L) Monroe Gilliken	Creeds Hill
CBM (L) Erskine Oden	Creeds Hill
BM1c (L) Thomas Barnett	Hatteras Inlet
Surfman Tommie G. Meekins	Hatteras Inlet
CBM (L) Levene W. Midgett	Hatteras Inlet
Surfman Guy G. Quidley	Hatteras Inlet
Surfman B.J. Scarborough	Hatteras Inlet
Surfman Sumner Scarborough	Hatteras Inlet
MoMM1c Dallas Williams	Hatteras Inlet

CBM (L) Levene Midgett, enlisted as a surfman in 1917, went on to serve as officer-in-charge of Chicamacomico LBSTA from 1937 to 1954, and retired after 37 years of service when the station closed.

Empire Gem Rescue – 1942

On 23 JAN 42 a British tanker, the *Empire Gem*, was bound for Britain via Halifax loaded with 10,600 tons of gasoline from Port Arthur. At that time she was the largest tanker in the world. As the ship approached Diamond Shoals it was torpedoed by a German U-boat, the *U-66*, about sixteen miles off Creeds Hill. A column of fire shot up 500 feet into the night sky when the torpedoes hit the vessel.

The Coast Guard had a lookout posted up in the Ocracoke Light twenty-four hours a day, and he spotted the explosion and flames from the burning tanker. The Ocracoke station's 36-foot motor lifeboat was sent out to the stricken vessel. The boat crew was made up of two veteran surfmen, BM1c (L) Olin Austin (coxswain) and MoMM1c (L) Harvey Wahab (engineer) from Ocracoke, and two recently enlisted seamen, Ulysses "Mack" Womack and Theodore Mutro. The run offshore

Captain and radio operator of British tanker, *Empire Gem*, Hatteras Inlet LBSTA, January 1942. They were the only survivors when their ship was torpedoed and sunk on 23 JAN 42 by *U-66* off Creeds Hill. Crew from this station rescued them in their 36-foot MLB. (Theodore Mutro)

from Ocracoke Inlet NE to Diamond Shoals took them four hours. When they reached the stricken vessel there was burning gasoline and debris all around in one huge fire. They searched in vain for survivors until their fuel ran low and they had to return to their station. The vessel burned to the water line before it sank.

The Hatteras Inlet station's 36-foot MLB also went out to assist, and they picked up the ship's captain and a radio operator and brought them safely back in to Hatteras Inlet LBSTA. All the rest of the ship's fifty-seven man British crew perished in the explosion and fire. Two years later, on 6 MAY 44, the *U-66* was sunk with a loss of 25 men after 40 months of service during which time it had sunk 29 ships.

At the time of this writing Theodore Mutro still lives in Ocracoke where he settled after leaving the Coast Guard. He was at Ocracoke LBSTA from early January of 1942 until July of 1943. He still clearly recalls that eventful day in 1942 when the *Empire Gem* exploded and went down, taking most of her crew with her. Before the war he was a seaman in the Merchant Marine on the tanker *Chester Sun*. In a strange twist of fate, on 10 MAR 42 his old ship sank off Big Kinnakeet.

Sadly , Ulysses "Mack" Womack, who also settled in Ocracoke after the war, died in February of 2000 before the author could interview him for this book. Both Mutro and Womack were also in the burial detail in 1942 when fallen British seamen were buried in the little British cemetery there in the village of Ocracoke.

Ocracoke LBSTA crew, March 1942. Left to right: CBM (L) Homer Gray (officer-in-charge)—Avon, BM1c (L) Olin Austin—Hatteras, BM1c (L) Ken Smith-Atlantic(?), SN Lockhard, SN Raymond Pabst—IL, SN Ross, SN Theodore Mutro—Chester, PA, SN A. T. Smith, SN Norman Stuber, SN Wright, SN Taylor, ?, SN Stoker, SN Ben Steckley—PA, SN Howard McHugh - MD . (Theodore Mutro)

MV *Norfolk* Rescue – 1948

On 7 MAR 48 a bad storm hit Atlantic Beach with strong SE winds, and heavy seas with huge breakers built up on the bar outside Beaufort Inlet. A sulfur ship, the MV *Norfolk*, ran aground on Beaufort Bar on its way into the inlet and called Fort Macon LBSTA for assistance. The station's 36-foot motor lifeboat got underway with a crew comprised of Reginald Lewis and Earl Johnson from Harkers Island, Percy Mason from Otway, and a veteran surfman, CMoMM (L) Carl Willis, who was also from Harkers Island. As the MLB attempted to run out of the inlet it encountered such high seas and poor visibility that it had to turn back. The boat broached-to and capsized in the turn when hit by a large breaker, and it rolled all the way over and then righted itself as it was designed to do. The boat's radio antenna was bent and Chief Willis broke three ribs when the boat rolled over. The MLB returned to the station to get medical assistance for the chief. The Cape Lookout MLB had also come out to assist, and they picked up one of the ship's crew who had jumped overboard. Due to the extremely rough seas and high winds the decision was made to wait until the weather calmed before attempting any further rescue action. The next morning it was still rough but had calmed some. The Fort

Rescue plaque, Group Fort Macon. At the time of this writing this plaque is still proudly displayed in the entrance hall of the group building. (Gerald Brebner)

Fort Macon LBSTA, ca. 1940. Masonry fort (built 1826-34) next to station property guarded Beaufort Inlet until 1924 when the Army abandoned it. It now a state historical site. (National Archives)

Macon MLB was found to be unserviceable because when it rolled over oil spilled and fouled the engine compartment so Cape Lookout LBSTA was requested to send their MLB back out. CBM (L) Wink Robertson from Atlantic, boat coxswain and OIC at Cape Lookout, came out in the Cape Lookout MLB and took the following men from Fort Macon LBSTA on the boat with him: seamen Stacy Davis from Harkers Island and Earl Styron as well as BM1c (L) Donald Willis, also from Harkers Island. When they reached the ship they got a line aboard which had a life ring tied to it with another line from the life ring to the MLB. Another line was passed to the ship, and the MLB was secured to the lee side of the ship's bow. They then had each member of the crew jump,one at the time, off the ship holding the life ring, and they proceeded to pick up each man from the water and get him into the MLB until the entire twenty-two man crew had been taken off the grounded vessel. They then ran back in to Fort Macon LBSTA, bringing everyone safely ashore. Later on the USCGC *Mendota* came up from Wilmington and tried to refloat the ship but was unsuccessful. A large oceangoing tug was then sent down from Norfolk and managed to pull the vessel off the bar. The grateful citizens of Coastal North Carolina presented Beaufort (Fort Macon) Group with a plaque expressing their gratitude for this rescue. At the time of this writing that plaque is still proudly displayed in the entrance hall of the Group Fort Macon main building.

Reginald Lewis went on to make chief boatswain's mate, and he retired in 1965. He was in the Navy on a fleet oiler during WW II. During his Coast Guard career he also served at Cape Lookout and Atlantic LBSTA's, and he was in the Group Fort Macon pulling boat race crew in the years 1948-51. He recalled wondering why they had a station at Atlantic in the late 1950's because "Drum Inlet was so shallow you couldn't float a shingle through it." .At the time of this writing he still lives on Harkers Island with his wife Madeline who has fond memories of when she first arrived at Harkers Island as a young bride from the big city and had to learn to adjust to her new life there.

Stacy Davis, who was in the Army during WW II in the Amphibious Forces as a landing craft coxswain, enlisted in the Coast Guard in 1947 and was released from active duty in 1950. He was assigned to Fort Macon Lifeboat Station and was in the Group Fort Macon pulling boat crew in the 1948 race off Cape Hatteras. He and Reginald Lewis are, at the time of this writing, the last surviving members of that boat crew. He went on to captain a Cedar Island-Ocracoke ferry and retired after 21 years of service. He and his wife Anna Kay still live at Harkers Island.

Fort Macon LBSTA, 14 FEB 50. Note edge of 1904 building between 1938 building and tower. Also note 26-foot MSB (left) and 36-foot MLB (center) on boat carriages on launchways. At the time of this writing boathouse (and equipment building behind it) are still in service here. Old station buildings were torn down ca.1965 to make room for new buildings. (National Park Service)

Omar Babun Rescue – 1954

On 13 May 54 a Honduran freighter, the *Omar Babun*, sailed from Philadelphia bound for Havana with a cargo of machinery, motors and steel. Early the next morning the vessel encountered high winds and rough seas off the North Carolina coast. Cargo broke loose and threatened to break down the stanchions supporting the deck. The captain then beached his ship for the safety of his crew. The freighter grounded in the surf some 250 feet offshore, around three miles north of Rodanthe and a mile and a half north of Mirlo Beach.

The ship sent a distress call on the radio at 1:05 AM., and patrols were sent out from the stations on Hatteras Island. Early in the morning on the 14th, before daylight, the ship was spotted by one of the crew from Chicamacomico LBSTA patrolling the beach. Crews from Cape Hatteras, Chicamacomico and Oregon Inlet LBSTA's came to the scene with their beach apparatus, and the rescue operation began at daylight. Using the breeches buoy the Coast Guardsmen brought the first crewman to shore at 7:50 AM, and by 9:45 AM all fourteen of the ship's crew were safely ashore. BMC Edward B. Midgett from Cape Hatteras LBSTA fired the line throwing gun and got a line out to the ship. The rescue operation was directed by Warrant Officer H.A. Glyn, the Coast Guard group commander. Ben Dixon Mac-Neill, retired newspaperman and author from Buxton, also came to the scene that day and worked with the Coast Guardsmen.

Many residents of Hatteras Island, including Ray Austin from Salvo, predicted that it would be impossible to refloat the *Omar Babun* or salvage any of her cargo. However, E.A. Canipe from Havelock thought differently, and he hired Austin to work on his salvage operation. Bulldozers built up a sand ramp covered with metal mats out to the ship, and trucks then were driven out to offload the cargo and haul it to Norfolk. Engines were set up on the ship's deck to run winches which took in lines run out to kedge anchors, and the ship was slowly refloated. She was taken in tow by a tug at high tide the evening of Sunday, July 18th, and towed to Norfolk.

This was the last breeches buoy rescue in North Carolina, and it marked the end of an era that had begun in the 1870's with the stations built by the U.S. Life-Saving Service. By the late 1950's the beach apparatus drill was being phased out, and breeches buoy rescues would be replaced by helicopter rescues. At the time of this writing, of the stations involved, only Oregon Inlet is still in commission, and a picture of this rescue is proudly displayed in the station building.

Last breeches buoy rescue in North Carolina, *Omar Babun*, Hatteras Island, 14 May 54. At the time of this writing this picture is still proudly displayed in Station Oregon Inlet. (Wayne Gray)

Omar Babun, Hatteras Island, summer of 1954. View of salvage operation undertaken by E. A. Canipe from Havelock. Ray Austin from Salvo operated the bulldozer in left background to build sand ramp out to the ship so it could be unloaded. Ship was refloated and towed away 7 JUL 54. (Outer Banks History Center)

British Cemeteries

HMT *Bedfordshire*, a 165-foot British armed trawler, was torpedoed and sunk by a German U-boat, the *U-558*, some forty miles south-southeast of Cape Lookout with the loss of all hands on 11 MAY 42. Days later Coast Guardsmen found the bodies of Sub-Lieutenant Thomas Cunningham and Telegraphist Second Class Stanley Craig in the surf on Ocracoke Island. They were taken to Ocracoke Lifeboat Station for identification and later buried with military honors in a small plot donated by the Williams family next to their own cemetery in Ocracoke. About a week after the burial two more bodies were found floating in the ocean. No identification could be made, but their clothing indicated they were British seamen. These two men were buried next to Cunningham and Craig. A little over a year later, on 20 JUL 43, the *U-558* was sunk with a loss of 44 men after 29 months in active service during which time it sank 20 ships.

Over the years Coast Guardsmen, individual civilians and various organizations have cared for the cemetery. In recent years British officials have attended a memorial ceremony on the Friday closest to May 11. The crew of Station Ocracoke to this day continues to care for the plot, and a British Union Jack still flies over the fallen sailors' graves.

British Cemetery, Ocracoke, February of 2000. Cemetery dates from 1942 and is cared for by Coast Guardsmen from Station Ocracoke and others. (author)

British cemetery, Ocracoke, 14 MAY 42. Burial of Sub-Lieutenant Thomas Cunningham, Royal Navy Volunteer Reserve, HMT *Bedfordshire*. Left to right: SN Theodore Mutro, CBM (L) Arnold Tolson, MoMM1c (L) Harvey Wahab. Also present were SN Harold "Okie" Oakland and SN Ulysses L. "Mack" Womack (National Park Service)

British Cemetery, Buxton, 7 JAN 2000. Here lie the remains of two fallen British seamen. Their bodies were found by the crew of Cape Hatteras LBSTA who buried them here near the station in 1942. (author)

There is another, lesser-known, British cemetery near another old Coast Guard station in North Carolina. In the early days of WW II, during the first six months of 1942, more than seventy ships were sunk off the North Carolina coast. In March and April U-boats sank ships at a rate of nearly one a day. Lifeboat station crewmen were kept busy out in their boats rescuing survivors and recovering bodies. On 9 APR 42, the British tanker *San Delfino* was torpedoed off Chicamacomico. Twenty-eight men died when their lifeboat drifted into the burning fuel. The body of Fourth Engineering Officer Michael Cairns from that tanker washed ashore near the Cape Hatteras Station and was found on 7 MAY 42. Men from the station held a funeral service for the fallen seaman and buried him near the station. Another British seaman's body, unidentified, washed up at Cape Hatteras and was found on 21 MAY 42. He was buried by the station crew next to Cairns. The two graves are marked by headstones and are fenced off. This small cemetery is in Buxton just off the Cape Point access road on the right before you get to the old station property and the campground. It is maintained by the Hatteras Island Historical Society, the Graveyard of the Atlantic Museum and the U.S. Coast Guard. The National Park Service is responsible for the integrity of the site.

Funeral service for Fourth Engineering Officer Michael Cairns (British Merchant Navy), Cape Hatteras LBSTA, May 1942. Left to right: Andrew Sterling, Pentacostal Church minister from Buxton; BM1c (L) Leonard Rollison from Frisco; BM1c (L) Columbus Miller from Avon,?, ?, ?, ?, ?, ?, CWO George Harrison Meekins (officer-in-charge) from Avon. (Wayne Gray)

Cape Hatteras Light, Coast Guard Day, 4 AUG 48. Crowd gathered for 5th District rowing team race. (Dalton Burrus)

August 4th Races

Before and after WW II rowing teams from lifeboat stations would race each other on Coast Guard Day (August 4th - the Coast Guard birthday). Buoys were placed to mark off the course. They would row their 26-foot self-bailing monomoy surfboats (pulling boats) 1/2 mile, capsize them, right them, get back aboard, take up their oars and pick up the stroke and row another 1/2 mile to complete the course. Men who rowed these boats jokingly said they had "Armstrong" engines. The boat crews trained hard for these races, and it was a matter of great pride among them to show what they could do in these races. Big crowds of onlookers watched the races, and they were very popular events every year among the local residents of the coastal areas where they were held.

Group Chincoteague rowing team, beach at Cape Hatteras Light, 4 AUG 48. Left to right: (kneeling) Charles Louis, Howard Parsons Jr., William Parker, Roland Powell; (standing) Jack Bunting, Forster Forbes, Wallace Bunting, John Munford, ? Mason. Forbes and Mason are North Carolinians, others are Marylanders, Mason was assigned to an 83-footer, others were assigned to Ocean City LBSTA. (Howard Parsons Jr.)

Coast Guard Day, Cape Hatteras Light, 4 AUG 48. Crowd gathered from up and down Hatteras Island and beyond for race between rowing teams from groups in the 5th Coast Guard District. Signal flags spell "Coast Guard Day 1790-1948." North Carolina's governor, R. Gregg Cherry, made a speech at this occasion extolling the heroism of the Coast Guard. (Dalton Burrus)

Pulling boat races between rowing teams from Groups Chincoteague, Virginia Beach, Cape Hatteras, and Fort Macon in the 5th District were held as follows:

Year	Location	Winner
1948	Cape Hatteras	Group Fort Macon
1949	Morehead City	Group Virginia Beach
1950	"Little" Washington	Group Fort Macon
1951	Elizabeth City	Group Fort Macon

The Morehead City Chamber of Commerce and the Morehead Rotary Club sponsored an awards dinner at the Blue Ribbon Club in Morehead City on 14 APR 49 to honor the Group Fort Macon boat crew, winners of the 1948 race. Ben Dixon MacNeill, well known North Carolina newspaperman and author, made the presentation speech, paying tribute to the "men with the oars." The Josephus Daniels Memorial Trophy was presented to BM1 (L) Walter Goodwin, the Fort Macon winning coxswain. This trophy was established by Josephus Daniels' sons (Josephus, Jr., Frank, Jonathan and Worth) to memorialize their father's lifetime interest in the Coast Guard.

Group Cape Hatteras rowing team in 26-foot pulling boat, practicing for annual race, Pamlico Sound off Buxton, 1949. At half way point of one mile course they are capsizing boat at coxswain's orders "Way enough" and "Capsize." Boat crew: BM1 (L) Dudley Burrus (coxswain), Orville Scarborough, Sumner Scarborough, Charlie Gray, R.C. Roy, Alston Tillett, ? Mitchell, Kermit Scarborough, and Lenwood Quidley. (Lenwood Quidley)

The winning time in the 1950 race was eight minutes and 20 seconds, Group Virginia Beach's second place time was less than two seconds behind that, and Group Cape Hatteras' third place time was less than one second behind second place. The crowd viewing the 1950 race at "Little" Washington was estimated at 10,000. VADM Merlin O'Neil, USCG Commandant, and North Carolina Congressman Herbert C. Bonner were among the dignitaries at the 1950 race.

These races between rowing teams from the different 5th District groups were discontinued after the 1951 race and, like other traditions from the Life-Saving Service era, have now passed into history.

Group Virginia Beach rowing team, Coast Guard Day, Cape Hatteras Light, 4 AUG 48. Salute with oars follows command "Toss oars." Left to right: (stern) BM1 (L) Woodrow Stetson (coxswain); (port side) Alston Meekins, Sidney Toler, David Farrow, Earl Midgett; (starboard side) "Tink" Scarborough, Carl Osmond, Irving Balance, Russell Dowdy. This crew was temporarily assigned the Chicamacomico LBSTA boat for this race. All are from North Carolina. (Dalton Burrus)

Start of pulling boat race, beach at Cape Hatteras Light, 4 AUG 48. The four boats are 5th Coast Guard District rowing teams from Groups Chincoteague, Virginia Beach, Cape Hatteras, and Fort Macon (winner). (Dalton Burrus)

Group Cape Hatteras/Cape Hatteras LBSTA/Cape Hatteras Loran STA, 1949. Left to right: (kneeling) SN Rasmussen, ?, SN Lewis Tarns, ?; (2nd row) BM3 Lenwood Quidley, ?, SN L. S. McDaniel, ?; (3rd row) ?, ?, ET2 Darlington, CS1 John L. Lewis; (4th row) SN Thomas Kelly, EN1(L) Vance Midgett, EN2 Moody Meekins, ENC (L) Otis Willis; (5th row) BMC (L) Creedon Midgett, CWBOSN George Harrison Meekins (GP CMDR), BMC (L) Lonnie Burrus. (Lenwood Quidley)

Group Fort Macon rowing team (winners of 4 AUG 48 boat race at Cape Hatteras), Blue Ribbon Club, Morehead City, 14 APR 49. Josephus Daniels Jr., presenting Daniels trophy to BM1 (L) Walter Goodwin, coxswain. Others, left to right: EN2 Early Merkley Johnson, SN Bertram (Stacy) Davis, SN Gerald Salter, SN Reginald Lewis, SN Earl Styron, SN Robert Hill, SN Bonnie Piner, CWO Harold Daniels (group commander), CWO George Meekins (previous group commander). At the time of this writing, Stacy Davis and Reginald Lewis are the only members of this boat crew who are still living. (Leta Styron)

Group Virginia Beach pulling boat, winner of Coast Guard Day race, Morehead City, 4 AUG 49. Crew: Sheldon O'Neal (coxswain),. "Tink" Scarborough, Carl Osmond, T. A. Meekins, Irving Balance, Durwood Miller, ?, ?, and C.D. Scarborough. ("Tink" Scarborough and Sheldon O'Neal)

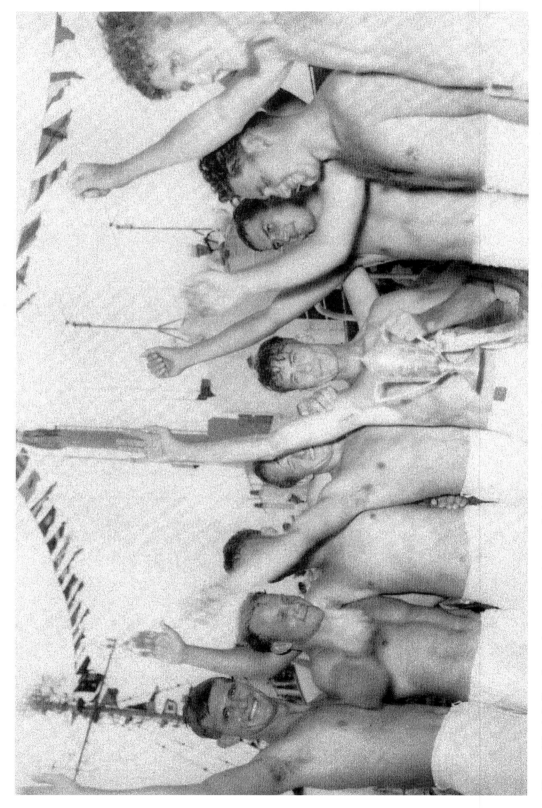

Group Virginia Beach rowing team, winners of 1949 race, Morehead City, 4 AUG 49. Left to right: "Tink" Scarborough, Carl Osmond, T. A. Meekins,?; Sheldon O'Neal (coxswain, holding trophy), Irving Balance, Durwood Miller, C.D. Scarborough. ("Tink" Scarborough and Sheldon O'Neal)

Group Cape Hatteras rowing team, Burnice's Creek, Buxton, 1951. Left to right: Dudley L. Burrus, Jasper E. Williams, Curtis L. Modlin, Maxton Scarborough, Johnny L. Williams, Kermit Scarborough, Avery M. Taylor, Orville Scarborough, Robert C. Roy, CWO George H. Meekins. (Johnny Williams)

CONCLUSION

All through the years right up to the present time North Carolinians have always done their duty serving steadfastly, as well as heroically whenever the need arose, at U.S. Life-Saving Service and U.S. Coast Guard stations. Many of those old stations are gone now. Pennys Hill, Poyners Hill, Paul Gamiels Hill, Nags Head, New Inlet, Gull Shoal, Big Kinnakeet, Cape Hatteras (first building) Hatteras Inlet (first, second, and third buildings), Ocracoke (first building), Atlantic , Fort Macon (first and second buildings), Cape Fear, and Oak Island (second building) long ago burned, washed down or were torn down. Wash Woods, Currituck Beach, Kitty Hawk (second building) Kill Devil Hills (first and second buildings), Pea Island (third building), Creeds Hill (second building), Durants, and Oak Island (first building) are privately owned at the time of this writing. Bodie Island, Little Kinnakeet, Cape Hatteras (second building), Portsmouth, and Cape Lookout are owned by the National Park Service. Ocracoke (second building) is still owned by the Coast Guard but its future is uncertain. Chicamacomico has been restored as a museum and is the most complete old station complex in North Carolina. Caffey's Inlet (second building) and Kitty Hawk (first building) are now restaurants. Oregon Inlet (second building) is in a sad state of disrepair now. Swansboro (second building) is still an active station. There are also, at the time of this writing, active small boat SAR stations at Oregon Inlet, Hatteras Inlet, Ocracoke, Fort Macon, Wrightsville Beach, and Oak Island.

Men who served in the old stations, as well as their families and their descendants, can rightfully be proud of the role they and those old stations played in the saving of so many lives down through the years. Names like Midgett, O'Neal, Daniels, Scarborough, Burrus, Gray, Etheridge, Meekins, Dowdy, Miller, Austin, and Williams will forever be linked to all the old lifesaving and lifeboat stations in North Carolina.

SEMPER PARATUS
(Always Faithful -Motto of the United States Coast Guard)

REFERENCES

BOOKS AND PERIODICALS:

Ballance, Alton. *Ocracokers*. Chapel Hill & London: The University of North-Carolina Press, 1989.

Chewning, Alpheus J. *The Approaching Storm – U-Boats off the Virginia Coast During World War II*. Lively, Virginia: Brandylane Publishers, 1994.

The Coast Guardsman's Manual. Annapolis: The United States Naval Institute, 1954.

Gannon, Michael. *Operation Drumbeat – The Dramatic True Story of Germany's First U-Boat Attacks Along The American Coast In World War II*. New York: Harper-Collins, 1991.

Hickam, Homer H. Jr. *Torpedo Junction – U-Boat War Off America's East Coast, 1942*. Annapolis: Naval Institute Press, 1989.

Johnson, Robert Erwin. *Guardians of the Sea – History of the United States Coast Guard, 1915 to the Present*. Annapolis: The United States Naval Institute, 1987.

McAdoo, Donald and Carol. *Reflections of the Outer Banks*. Manteo: Island Publishing House, 1976.

MacNeill, Ben Dixon. *The Hatterasman*. Winston-Salem: John F. Blair, 1958.

MacNeill, Ben Dixon. *Sand Roots*. Winston-Salem: John F. Blair, 1963.

Mobley, Joe A. *Ship Ashore! – The U.S. Lifesavers of Coastal North Carolina*. Raleigh: North Carolina Division of Archives and History, 1994.

Naisawald, L. VanLoan. *In Some Foreign Field – Four British Graves and Submarine Warfare on the North Carolina Outer Banks*. Raleigh: North Carolina Division of Archives and History, 1997.

Shanks, Ralph, Wick York and Lisa Woo Shanks, editor. *The U.S. LifeSaving Service, Heroes, Rescues and Architecture of the Early Coast Guard*. Petaluma, CA: Costano Books, 1996.

Scheina, Robert L. *U.S. Coast Guard Cutters & Craft of World War II*. Annapolis: The United States Naval Institute, 1982.

Stick, David. *Bald Head - A History of Smith Island and Cape Fear.* Wendell, NC: Broadfoot Publishing Company, 1985.

Stick, David. *Graveyard of the Atlantic.* Chapel Hill: The University of North Carolina Press, 1952.

Wechter, Nell Wise. *The Mighty Midgetts of Chicamacomico.* Manteo, NC: The Times Printing Co., 1974

NEWSPAPERS

The Carolina Coast (The Virginian-Pilot & The Ledger Star), May 15, 1988.

Coastland Times (Manteo), May 21, 1954.

News and Observer (Raleigh), May 15, 1954; July 21, 1954.

GOVERNMENT DOCUMENTS

Annual Report of the United States Coast Guard. Washington: U.S. Government Printing Office, 1915.

Logbook, Chicamacomico Lifeboat Station, U.S. Coast Guard. August 16, 1918.

Logbook, Hatteras Inlet Lifeboat Station, U.S. Coast Guard. December 9-10, 1931.

Register Of The Commissioned and Warrant Officers And Cadets, And Ships And Stations Of The United States Coast Guard. Washington: U.S. Government Printing Office, 1940.

U.S. Coast Guard Bulletin, CG 134, Volume 4, Number 11, May 1949.

INDEX

26-foot Pulling Boat (Monomoy Surfboat) 33, 34, 39, 44, 73, 79
26-foot Motor Surfboat (MSB) 36, 47, 66, 73, 74
30-foot Rescue Boat 74, 77
36-foot Motor Lifeboat (MLB) 66, 69, 70, 73, 74, 80, 87, 88, 89,. 91, 93
38-foot Cabin Picket Boat 38, 66, 67, 87
41-foot Utility Boat (UTB) 72
44-foot Motor Lifeboat (MLB) 70
45-foot Buoy Boat 67
47-foot Motor Lifeboat (MLB) 72, 73
82-foot Patrol Boat 72
83-foot Patrol Boat 67, 103
110-foot Patrol Boat 72

A

Anna May 54, 65, 85, 87
Ash Wednesday Storm (March 6 & 7, 1962) 20, 28, 31, 32, 42
Askins Creek 51
Atlantic Beach 72, 91
Atlantic Lifeboat Station (LBSTA) 68, 69, 93
Austin, Donald 64
Austin, Edward 64
Austin, John R. 88
Austin, Olin 88, 90
Austin, Ray 95, 97
Austin, Robert L. 12
Austin, Willie A. 12
Austin, Willie H. 58, 87
Avon 33, 51, 101

B

Ballance, Bernice R. 87, 88
Ballance, Irving 107, 111, 112
Barnett, Dave 52
Barnett, Loran 53
Barnett, Thomas 88
Barnett, W.L. 54
Beach Apparatus Drill 59
Beach Patrol 68, 78
Beacham, J. L. 21
Beacham, Walter 19
Beasley, James B. 12
Beasley, Sammie E. 15
Beasley, Samuel B. 15
Beaufort Bar 91
Beaufort Inlet 91, 92
Berry, Maxi 41

Big Kinnakeet Lifeboat Station (LBSTA) 51
Billard, RADM Frederick C. 83, 84
Black Pelican Restaurant 23
Blue Ribbon Club (Morehead City) 110
Bodie Island 36
Bodie Island Lifeboat Station (LBSTA) 35, 36
Bodie Island Light 35
Bogue Banks 74
Bogue Inlet 74
Bonner, Herbert C. 106
Bowden, Caleb C. 15
Bowser, Benjamin 43
Breeches Buoy 1, 95
Breeches Buoy Rescue 95, 96
Brewster (steamer) 54, 58
Britain 88
British Cemetery 89, 98, 99, 100
Brothers, Clayton 64
Bunting, Jack 103
Bunting, Wallace 103
Burrus, Dalton 75
Burrus, Dudley L. 105, 113
Burrus, Lonnie 109
Buxton 95, 100, 101, 105, 113

C

Caffeys Inlet Lifeboat Station (LBSTA) 18, 19, 20, 33
Cairns, Michael 100, 101
Canipe, E. A. 95, 97
Cape Fear 1
Cape Fear Lifeboat Station (LBSTA) 78
Cape Hatteras 1, 54, 56, 58, 65, 85, 93, 100
Cape Hatteras Loran Station 109
Cape Hatteras Lifeboat Station (LBSTA) 33, 53, 55, 56, 85, 87, 95, 100, 101, 109
Cape Hatteras Lifesaving Station 52
Cape Hatteras Light 52, 53, 54, 102, 103, 104, 105, 107
Cape Lookout 1, 98
Cape Lookout Lifeboat Station (LBSTA) 69, 70, 71, 93
Cape Lookout Light 51, 58, 69
Cape Lookout MLB 93
Cape Lookout National Seashore 68, 69
Cape Point 53, 100
Cedar Island 93
Chester Sun (tanker) 89
Chicamacomico Historical Association 47
Chicamacomico Lifeboat Station (LBSTA) 33, 46, 47, 48, 81, 82, 83, 84, 88, 95

Corbell, Malachi 13
Core Bank 68, 69
Corolla 5, 13, 14, 17, 25
Craig, Stanley 98
Creeds Hill 88, 89
Creeds Hill Lifeboat Station (LBSTA) 57, 58, 85
Croatan Inn 27
Cunningham, Sub-Lieutenant Thomas, RNVR 98, 99
Currituck Beach Lifeboat Station (LBSTA) 14, 15, 16
Currituck Beach Light 14, 16

D

Dailey, Benjamin B. 54
Dailey, John H. 54
Daniels, Frank 105
Daniels, Harold 110
Daniels, Jonathan 105
Daniels, Josephus, Jr. 105, 110
Daniels, Worth 105
Davis, Josh J. 52
Davis, Stacy 93, 110
Dough, Thomas E. 31, 33, 34
Dowdy, C. C. 21
Drum Inlet 69, 93
Duck 18, 21
DUKW (amphibious truck) 25, 27, 29, 32, 33, 34, 46
Durants Lifeboat Station (LBSTA) 58, 59
Durants Station (motel) 58, 59

E

E. S. Newman (schooner) 43
Elizabeth City 105
Empire Gem (tanker) 88, 89
Ephraim Williams (barkentine) 54, 58
Etheridge, Patrick H. 52, 58
Etheridge, Richard 43
Etheridge, Walter G. 85

F

Farrow, David 33, 107
Forbes, Forster 103
Fort Caswell 79
Fort Macon Lifeboat Station (LBSTA) 33, 72, 73, 91, 92, 93, 94
Fort Macon MLB 91, 93
Frisco 57, 58, 101
Fulcher, Charles E. 54
Fulcher, D. E. 58
Fulcher, Doc 19
Fulcher, James W. 69

G

Gaskill, William H. 69
Gaskins, V.O. 58
Gilliken, Monroe 88
Glyn, H.A. 95
Gold Lifesaving Medal 13, 43, 47, 49, 54, 58, 69, 83
Goodwin, Walter 105, 110
Graveyard of the Atlantic Museum 100
Gray, Charlie 105
Gray, Homer 90
Gray, Thomas 54
Gray, Wesley 64
Group Cape Hatteras 53, 105, 106, 108, 109, 113
Group Chincoteague 103, 105, 108
Group Fort Macon 72, 73, 91, 93, 105, 108, 110
Group Virginia Beach 105, 106, 107, 108, 111, 112
Gull Shoal Lifeboat Station (LBSTA) 48, 49
Guthrie, John 69
Guthrie, Kilby 69
Guthrie, Luther 70

H

Halifax 88
Harkers Island 70, 91, 93
Harris, Aubrey 19
Harris, Bill 79
Harris, Thomas J. "Jep" 38, 85, 86
Hatteras Inlet 87
Hatteras Inlet Lifeboat Station (LBSTA) 60, 61, 62, 63, 64, 65, 85, 89
Hatteras Island 65, 95, 104
Hatteras Island Historical Society 100
Havana 95
Haywood, Manie 21
Henley, Peter T. 15
Hill, Robert 110
HMT *Bedfordshire* (armed trawler) 98
Hooper, Basil 64

I

Irving, William 43

J

Jarvis, Calupt T. 69
Jennett, Baxter 88
Jennett, Issac L. 52, 54
Jennett, Jabez B. 54
Jennette, Leon 64
Johnson, Earl Merkley 91, 110
Johnson, Jessie J. 15
Jones, Howard 33
Jones Hill 16
Josephus Daniels Memorial Trophy 105

K

Kelly, Thomas 109
Ketcham, James M. 88
Kill Devil Hills 85
Kill Devil Hills Lifeboat Station (LBSTA) 7, 25, 26, 28, 29, 33, 85, 86
Kirkman, John E. 69
Kitty Hawk 21, 23, 33
Kitty Hawk Lifeboat Station (LBSTA)23, 85
Kitty Hawk Lifesaving Station 23
Kyzikes (tanker) 85

L

"L" Men 5
Lewark, Lewis L. 15
Lewark, Will H. 85, 86
Lewis, Jimmie 70
Lewis, John L. 109
Lewis, Joseph L. 69
Lewis, Reginald 91, 93, 110
Lifesaving Branch (USCG) 5
Life-Saving Service 1
Little Kinnakeet Lifeboat Station (LBSTA) 50, 51
"Little" Washington 105, 106
Lockerman, Howard C.79
Long Beach 79
Louis, Charles 103
Lyle Gun 1

M

MacNeill, Ben Dixon 53, 95, 105
McDaniel, L. S. 109
Manteo 33, 84
Mason, Jack 75
Mason, Percy 91
Meekins, Alston 33, 107
Meekins, George Harrison 54, 101, 109, 110, 113
Meekins, Moody 109
Meekins, T. A.111, 112
Meekins, Theodore 43, 52
Meekins, Tommy G. 87, 88
Midgett, Arthur V. 47, 83, 84
Midgett, Bannister III 81
Midgett, Chesley 36
Midgett, Clarence E. 47, 48, 83, 84
Midgett, Creedon 109
Midgett, E.J. 54
Midgett, Earl 33, 107
Midgett, Earlie 15
Midgett, Edgar 33
Midgett, Edward B. 64, 95
Midgett, Hurbert 36
Midgett, John Allen Jr. 47, 81, 82, 83, 84
Midgett, John H. 52, 54

Midgett, Leroy S.47, 48, 83, 84
Midgett, Levene W. 39, 65, 81, 87, 88
Midgett, O. O. 54
Midgett, Paul 30, 33, 34
Midgett, Rasmus S. 49
Midgett, T. S. 21
Midgett, Truxton E. 19
Midgett, Vance 109
Midgett, Woodson 12
Midgett, Zion S 47, 83, 84
Miller, Baxter B. 52, 54
Miller, Columbus 101
Miller, Durwood 111, 112
Miller, Frank W. 88
Miller, H.S. 54
Mirlo (tanker) 47, 48, 81, 82, 84
Mirlo Beach 95
Mitchell, Evans E. 38
Modlin, Curtis L. 113
Moore, Tyre 69
Morehead City 105, 110, 111
Morehead City Chamber of Commerce 105
Morehead City Rotary Club 105
Morris, Troy 12
Motor Machinist's Mate ("motor mac") 5
Munford, John 103
Mutro, Theodore 88, 89, 90, 99
MV *Norfolk* (sulfur ship) 91

N

Nags Head Lifeboat Station (LBSTA) 30, 31, 32, 33, 34, 85
National Park Service 35, 36, 43, 47, 50, 51, 53, 56, 68, 69, 100
New Inlet 45, 49
New Inlet Lifeboat Station (LBSTA) 45
Norfolk 93
North Carolina Aquarium (Manteo) 43
North Carolina Maritime Museum 69

O

Oak Island 79
Oak Island Lifeboat Station (LBSTA) 79, 80
Ocean City LBSTA 103
Ocracoke (village) 65, 68, 88, 89
Ocracoke Inlet 89
Ocracoke Island 60, 61, 62, 65, 98
Ocracoke Lifeboat Station (LBSTA) 65, 66, 67, 76, 85, 87, 88, 89, 90, 98
Ocracoke Light 88
Oden, Erskine 88
Old Currituck Inlet 14
Olds, Willouby 19
Olsen, Charlie 52

Omar Babun (freighter) 95, 96, 97
O'Neal, Edgar 7
O'Neal, Prochorus L. 47, 83, 84
O'Neal, Sheldon 9, 111, 112
Oregon Inlet Lifeboat Station (LBSTA) 9, 31, 33, 35, 36, 37, 38, 39, 40, 86, 95, 96
Osmond, Carl 107, 111, 112
Outer Diamonds 54, 58, 65, 85, 87, 88

P

Pamlico Sound 105
Parker, William 103
Parsons, Howard Jr. 103
Paul Gamiels Hill Lifeboat Station (LBSTA) 21, 22
Pea Island 36, 40
Pea Island Lifeboat Station (LBSTA) 41, 42, 44
Pea Island National Wildlife Refuge 41
Peel, Eugene H. 58
Peel, Ira 33
Pennys Hill Lifeboat Station (LBSTA) 14, 16
Philadelphia 95
Piner, Bonnie 110
Port Arthur 88
Portsmouth Island 68
Portsmouth Lifeboat Station (LBSTA) 68
Powell, Roland 103
Poyners Hill Lifeboat Station (LBSTA) 16, 17, 18
Priscilla (barkentine) 49
Pugh, Dorman 43

Q

Quagmires Restaurant 27
Quidley, Guy C. 87, 88
Quidley, Lenwood 105, 109
Quidley, Preston 64

R

Revenue Cutter Service 1
Robertson, Wink 93
Robinson, Donald T. 75
Rodanthe 47, 95
Rollison, Leonard 101
Roy, Robert C. 105, 113

S

Salter, Gerald 110
Salvo 41, 49, 95, 97
San Delfino (tanker) 100
Sanderlin, Jennings B. 15
Sanderling Inn Resort and Conference Centre 18, 20
Sarah D. J. Rawson (schooner) 69

Scarborough, B. J. 88
Scarborough, C. D. 111, 112
Scarborough, D. O. 21
Scarborough, Edward 64
Scarborough, Ignatius 12
Scarborough, Kermit 105, 113
Scarborough, Maxton 113
Scarborough, Orville 105, 113
Scarborough, Richard 87
Scarborough, Sumner M. 87, 88
Scarborough, "Tink" 107, 111, 112
Silver Lake 65
Silver Lifesaving Medal 31, 54, 65
Simmons, E. A. 21
Smith, Ken 90
Smith (Bald Head) Island 78
Snow, G. G. 21
Sterling, Andrew 101
Sterling, John E. 8
Stetson, Woodrow 107
Stowe, Ed 52
Styron, Augustus W. 12
Styron, Earl 93, 110
Styron, Earnest 64
Surfboats 1
Surfmen 5
Swansboro LBSTA 74, 75, 76, 77

T

Tarns, Lewis 109
Taylor, Avery M. 113
Tillett, A. D. 21
Tillett, Melvin 19
Toler, Sidney C. 33, 107
Tommys Hummock 35
Twiford, William T. 12

U

U-66 88, 89
U-117 81
U-558 98
USCGC *Block Island* 72
USCGC *Elm* 72
USCGC *Mendota* 93
USCGC *Midgett* 83
USCGC *Primrose* 72
USCGC *Staten Island* 72

W

Wahab, Harvey 88, 89
Wash Woods Lifeboat Station (LBSTA) 12, 13
Wescott, Lewis 43
Wescott, R. L. 21

Whale Head 16
Whalehead Club 14, 17
Williams, Dallas 85, 87, 88
Williams, Jasper E. 113
Williams, Johnny 64, 113
Williams, Raymond L. 12
Williams, Urias 52
Williams, U. B. 54
Willis, Carl 91
Willis, Donald 93
Willis, Earl 7

Willis, Jackie 64
Willis, Otis 109
Wilmington 93
Wise, Stanley 43
Womack, Ulysses L. "Mack" 88, 89, 99
Wroten, Ben 8

Y

Yeomans, Walter M. 69

ADDENDUM I

The Boathouse at Hatteras Inlet

(This incident was shared with the author by Dalton Burrus, a Hatterasman, during a visit with him and his wife Ruby, in December of 1999.)

In July of 1950 Dalton was a boatswain's mate second class, assigned to Hatteras Inlet LBSTA on the north end of Ocracoke Island. The shoreline was migrating so near to the main station building that it was at risk of washing into the sea. The district office decided to enlarge the boathouse (built 1940) and move the crew there. Work was almost finished – a new galley, mess room, office and sleeping quarters. Plans were being made to move in very soon.

One morning the rowing team comprised of Dalton and three other men left for Ocracoke LBSTA where they were to practice with five of their men in preparation for the pulling boat competition coming up in August. When they arrived around 0800 the chief informed them that the boathouse at Hatteras Inlet was on fire. They picked up a P-500 pump, put it in back of their truck, and immediately headed back to their station. When they arrived the boathouse was engulfed in flames, and there was no chance of saving anything. Their 36-foot motor lifeboat and 26-foot motor surfboat were destroyed along with the entire building.

The district office in Norfolk was notified of the disaster, and they dispatched a captain in a seaplane to investigate. The seaplane landed about 1,000 yards off from the site. Dalton and another man rowed the 19-foot dory out to pick up the plane passengers. When they came alongside the plane the captain was standing in the doorway. Dalton warned him to be careful because the dory was tricky. He informed Dalton that he had been in dories before Dalton was born. He then stepped out onto the gunnel, the dory capsized, and all three were dumped in the water.

The boathouse was never rebuilt. A few years after the fire the station was relocated to Hatteras Island.

ADDENDUM II

(excerpts from *THE COAST GUARDSMAN'S MANUAL* – 1954 edition)

Surfmanship

Rowing to seaward.--The two important principles in the operation are: (1) keep the bow directly into the seas; and (2) keep sufficient way on the boat to prevent its being stopped and carried shoreward by a breaker. If the latter happens, the boat will most certainly broach-to and capsize. (*Broaching-to* is the action wherein a boat is turned broadside to the seas. This almost invariably happens if a boat is carried along on the front of a breaker for any distance.) Therefore, getting good headway on the boat and maintaining it through the breakers is essential in most cases. By watching the seas beyond the breaker line, a good coxswain can pick a period when smaller breakers will be coming in, and can time his passage so the boat will meet these smaller breakers on the way out.

Rowing to the beach through a surf.—From seaward, a surf always looks smaller than it is in actuality. Therefore, an inexperienced crew should always approach the breaker line cautiously and lie to for a while to observe the surf. If the surf is comparatively calm, commence rowing towards the beach *stern first*. Once inside the breaker line, the boat is kept underway going astern; but upon the approach of a breaker, the crew stops rowing astern and pulls ahead with all the speed they can muster so that the boat has good headway by the time the breaker meets it. As soon as the breaker passes under the boat, the crew rows astern again until another breaker approaches, whereupon they pull ahead again. This process is continued until the beach is reached. When rowing ahead to meet a breaker, the same two principles of keeping the bow directly into the seas and having sufficient headway must be observed as in the case of making the passage from the beach to seaward....

NOTES